Stroll

Balthazar Lovay (ed.)

jrp|ringier

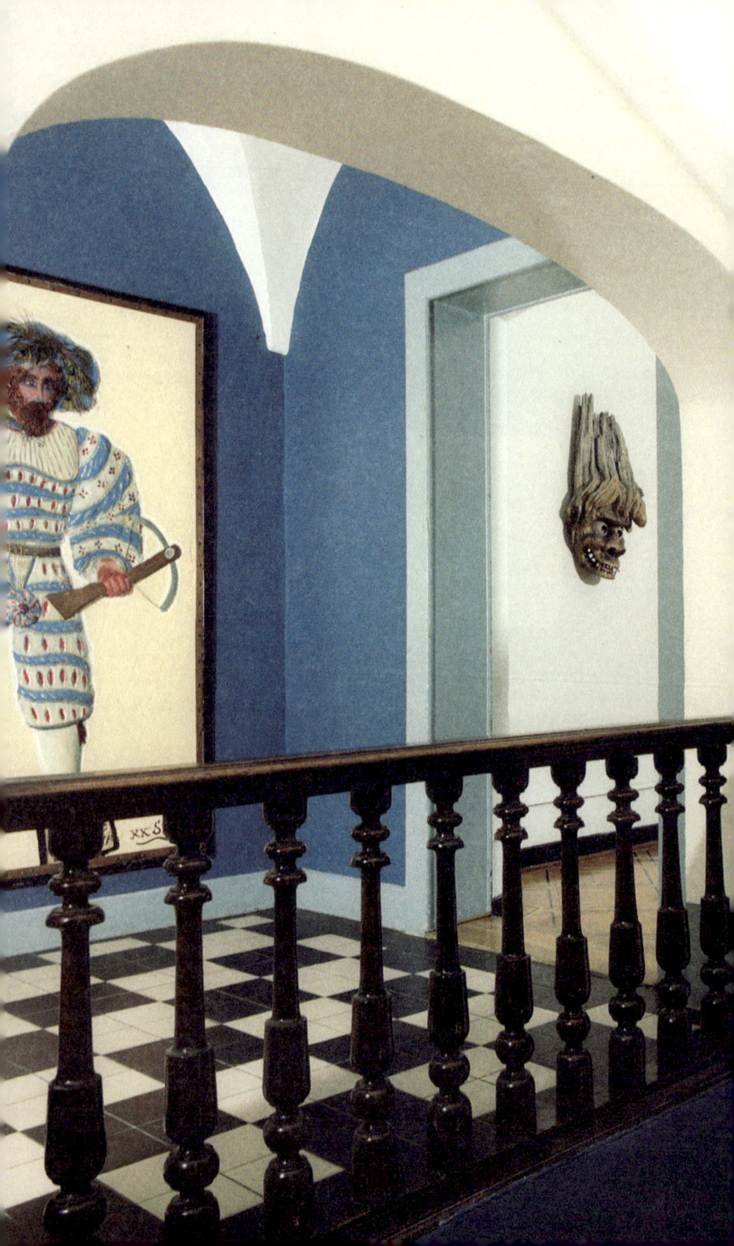

Table of Contents

7   A Curatorial Experiment

13   Adventures, Reflections, and Ambushes
A Conversation Between Daniel Baumann
and Balthazar Lovay

52   List of Works

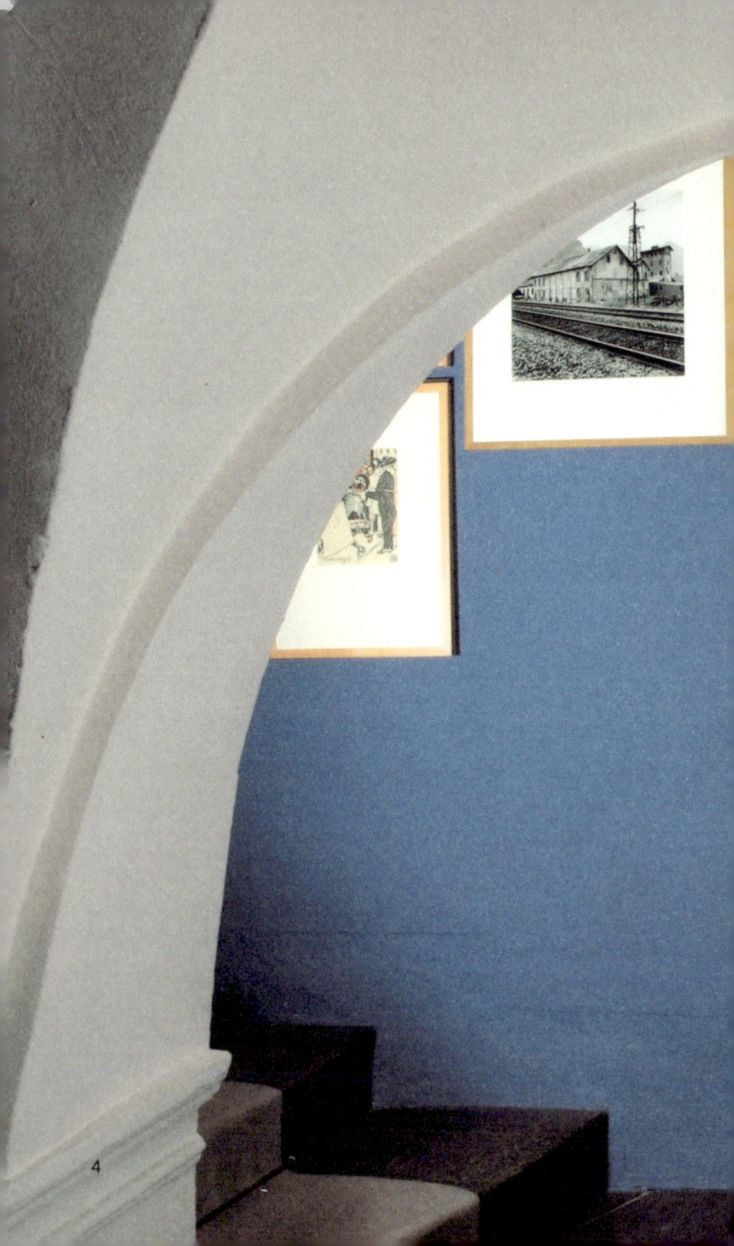

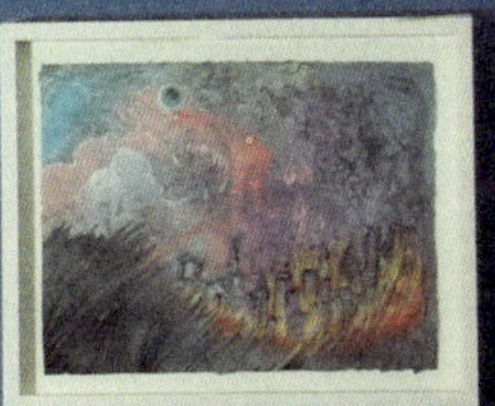

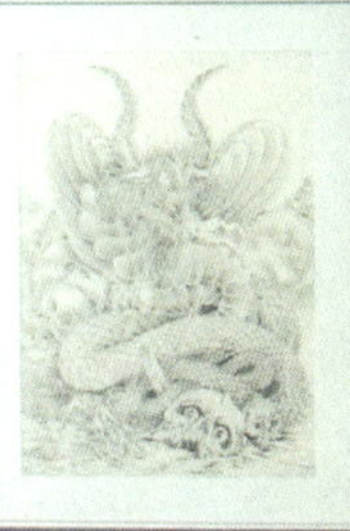

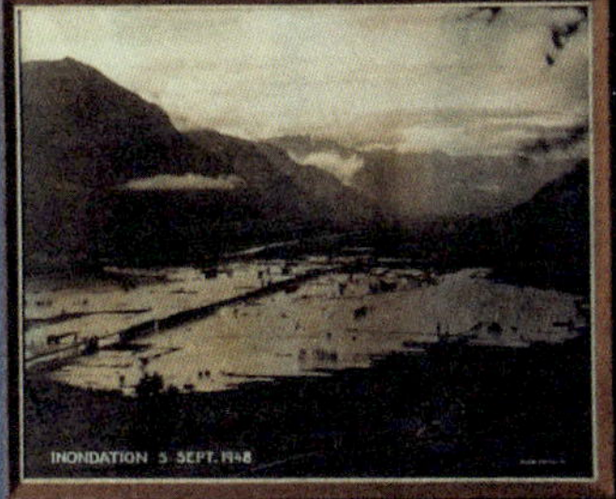

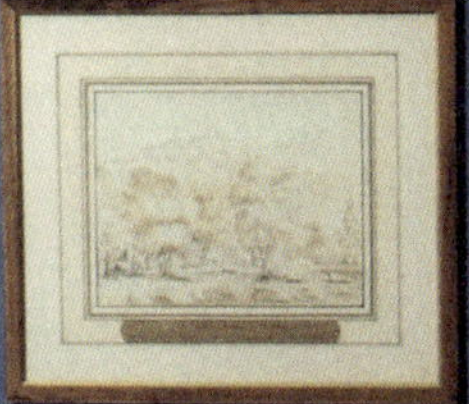

Exhibition view, "Fantastic Parophrenia" section

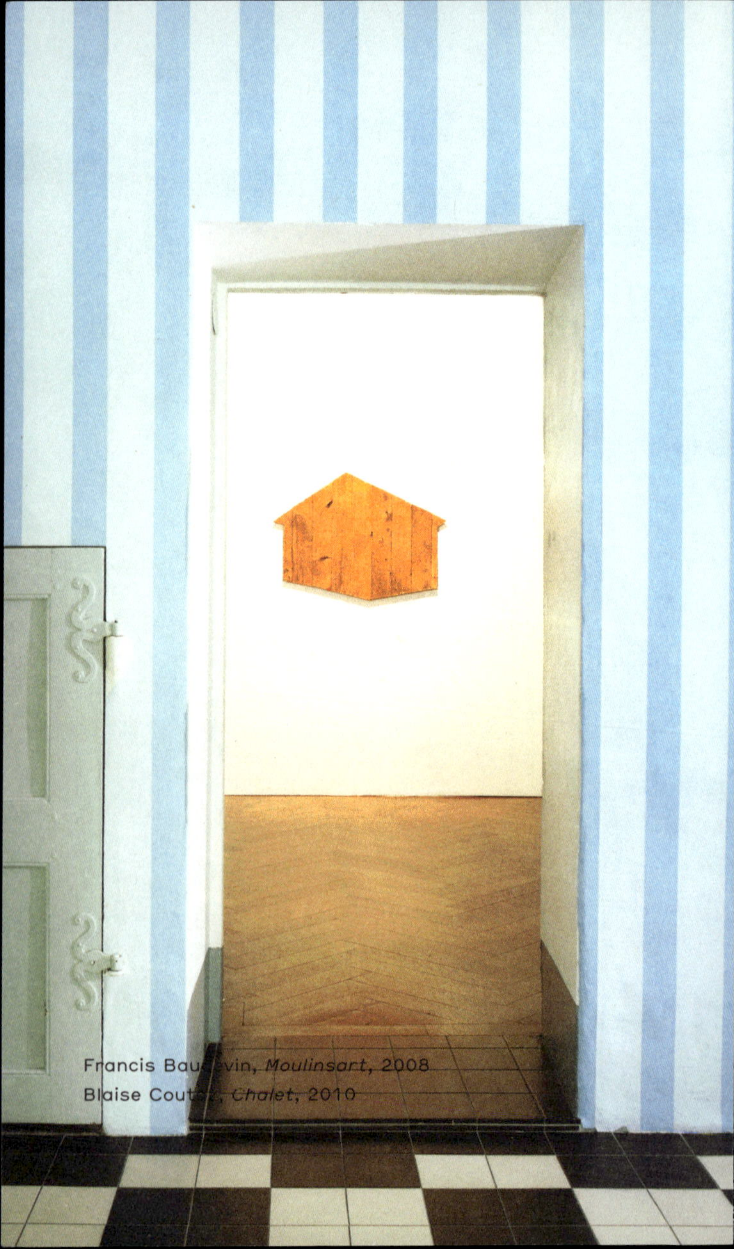

Francis Bauchevin, *Moulinsart*, 2008
Blaise Couté, *Chalet*, 2010

A Curatorial Experiment

How to think about and make a group exhibition today?

This is one of the questions that arose when Balthazar Lovay was invited in fall 2011 to conceive of an exhibition for the Manoir de Martigny, a 17th-century building located in a little town at the foot of the Swiss Alps.

This book, in the appropriately-titled Hapax series—"hapax" meaning a word or a form that occurs only once in the recorded corpus of a given language—is the literary extension of the exhibition *Adventures, Reflections, and Ambushes*, which was somehow also a hapax. Because Balthazar Lovay decided to create an exhibition in the form of a mental universe in which left and right cerebral cortexes could at last communicate with each other, this show is both highly personal and eminently universal. Each visitor and each reader can thus appropriate the works and the artifacts gathered here with their own feelings toward and apprehension of art, aesthetics, and images. The exhibition was conceived in a transversal and non-authoritarian manner, creating successive sections such as "Fantastic Paraphrenia," "Mental Landscape," and "A Forest of Signs," and using an old-fashioned hanging style. Juxtaposing the artworks of 60 international and local artists, photographers, and press cartoonists, the exhibition unites such different fields as contemporary art, modern art, self-taught art, medieval statuary, so-called "art brut," and vernacular culture. For instance, Max Ernst's series of engravings entitled *Histoire naturelle (Natural History)* converses with carnival masks; New-York-based artists Guyton\Walker are hung next to a 14th-century polychrome reclining Christ.

In the current landscape of group exhibitions, *Adventures, Reflections, and Ambushes* assumes a free and atypical position, raising questions rather than offering answers, proposing new perspectives on art history. This project was constructed from the ground up: each carefully chosen artifact participates with its own distinct voice in a polyphonic constellation, thus allowing visitors to perceive a very idiosyncratic vision (that of the curator) just as they are invited to build their own. What happens if Ian Wilson's last tangible sculpture is shown next to a multi-dimensional work by Steven Parrino? If the hidden treasures of the Manoir de Martigny's Collection dialogue with the new New York art scene? While all these "chance encounters" are offered to the viewer, it becomes clear that the pairing of works was far from being random. Neither thematic nor historical nor market-oriented, this exhibition is perhaps all these things simultaneously.

This introduction could have also started the other way around, inviting you to read this text as the visitor enters the Manoir de Martigny on a sunny fall afternoon. On the threshold, you face the first staircase of the Manoir, from where dozens of artworks from different times and techniques stare at you. Then, climbing the stairs and reading the conversation between Balthazar Lovay and Daniel Baumann on the following pages, you could start to understand what the exhibition wanted to make you feel, being able to choose between a synthetic vision of the show and a precise look to each work, paying the same attention to a conceptual device as to a vernacular object or a political cartoon. All these possibilities are equivalent. Indeed, they are recommended in order to roam between the proposals and accidents of this curatorial experiment.

Artists in the Exhibition

Josse Bailly
Francis Baudevin
Hans Bellmer
A. Bessi
Jacques Berthet
Edmond Bille
Kim Seob Boninsegni
Abraham Bosse
Michel Bovisi
Rodolphe Bresdin
Marguerite Burnat-Provins
Julien Carreyn
Valentin Carron
Achille Chappaz
Blaise Coutaz
Stéphane Dafflon
Oscar Darbellay
Andreas Dobler
Préfète Duffaut
Cédric Eisenring
Max Ernst
Vidya Gastaldon
Alberto Giacometti
H.R. Giger
Marie-Antoinette Gorret
Michel Grillet
Guyton\Walker
Mamie Holst
Alex Hubbard
Hayan Kam Nakache
Michael Kimber

Norbert H. Kox
Dominique Lang
Pierre Loye
Tobias Madison
François Morellet
Robert Morris
Gianni Motti
Charles-Clos Olsommer
Steven Parrino
Seth Price
Punk
Joseph Domenico Rabiato
R.M. Ramagli
Agnes Rieder Wiler
Marta Riniker-Radich
Félicien Rops
Emanuel Rossetti
Bertram Schoch
Jim Shaw
David Shrigley
Moritz Siegen
Skyll
Josh Smith
Louis Soutter
Elvis Studio
Olivier Taramarcaz
Éric Vuille
Ludwig Werlen
Ian Wilson
Mirza Zwissig

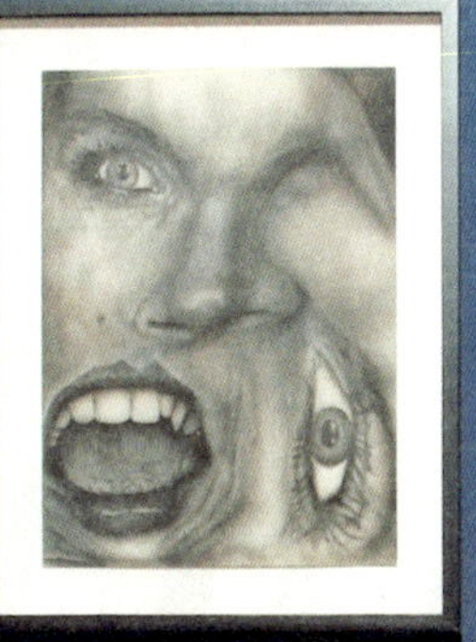
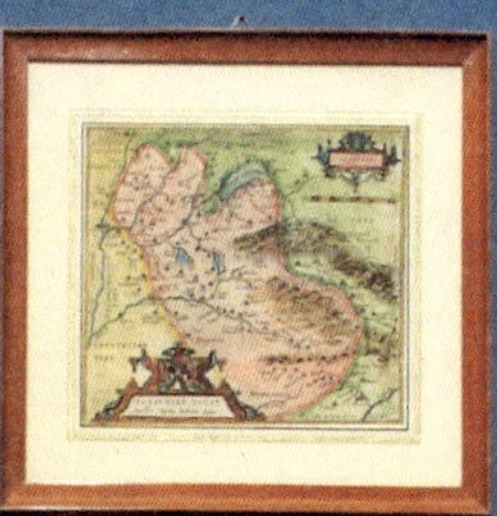
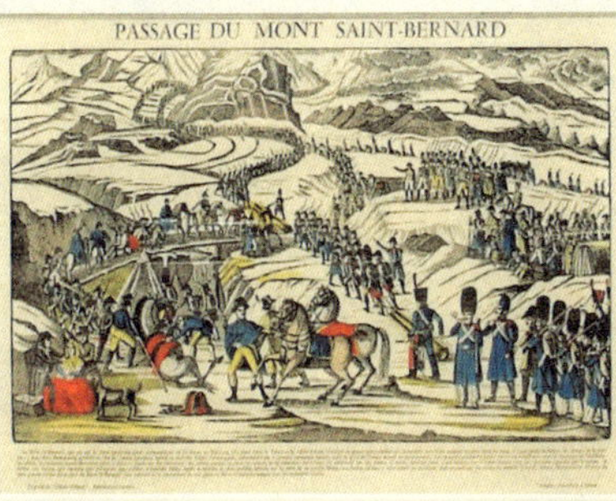

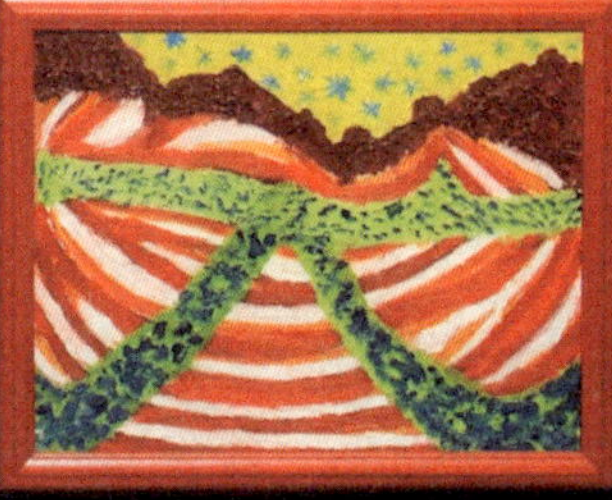

Exhibition view, "Fantastic Paraphrenia" section

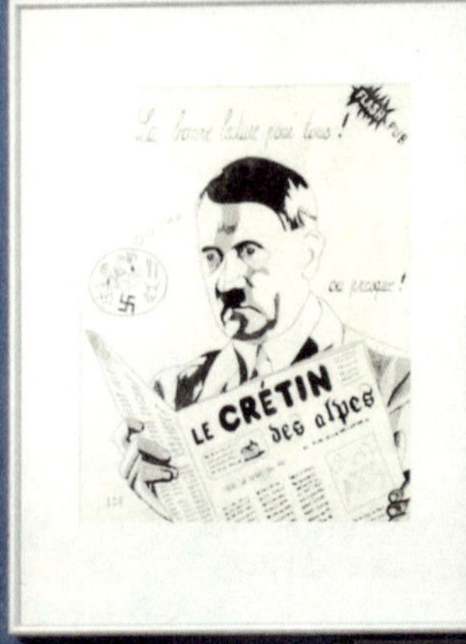

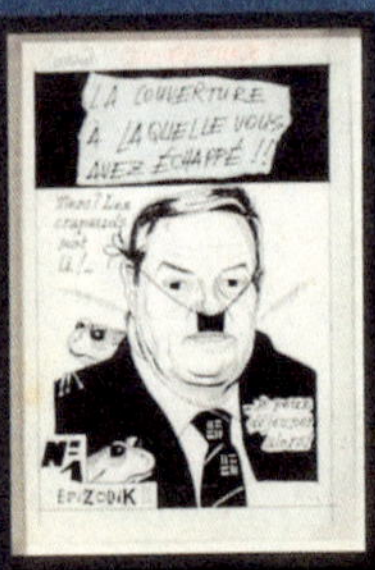

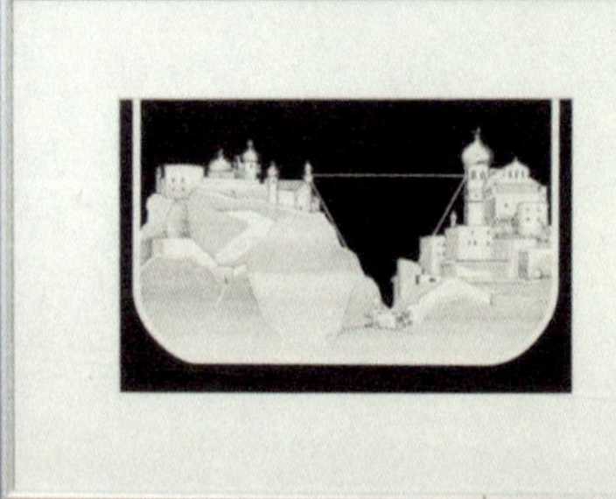

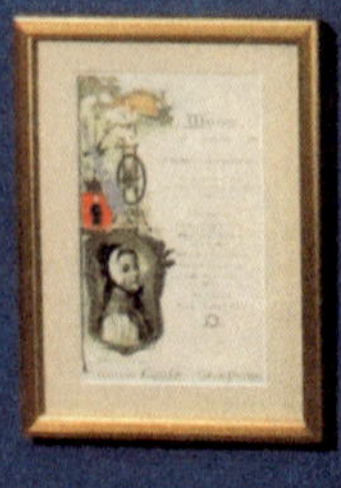

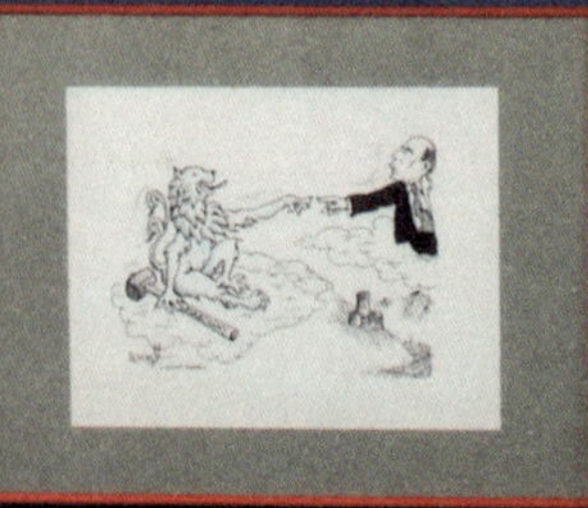

Exhibition view, "Fantastic Paraphrenia" section

12

Adventures, Reflections, and Ambushes

A Conversation Between Daniel Baumann
and Balthazar Lovay

DB — How did the *Adventures, Reflections, and Ambushes* exhibition come about?

BL — Mads Olesen, the director of the Manoir de la Ville de Martigny, invited me to curate an exhibition. He conceives of this space more as a cultural center than as a museum; he organizes ethnographic exhibitions here, as well as retrospectives, festivals, etc. He takes a transversal approach to culture.

DB — Which is also our approach, isn't that right? How did you proceed in concrete terms? A transversal approach can quickly become an arbitrary approach, the risk being to end up as a multicultural stew, a big load of nonsense.

BL — I envisioned the project in the freest way possible, without thematic or stylistic constraints. I let myself be carried along by a kind of Debordian "dérive," by visiting specialized contemporary art collections, local artists, history museums, and by leafing through forgotten

stacks of old art catalogues. It was then necessary to get the various selected objects to
speak to each other. The result creates con-
frontations or, more precisely, situations. These
are not directive, but open and suggestive.
Hence, on the surface, there is an exhibition
that could be the image of my personal museum
and, in an underlying way, a more general ques-
tioning about art. Most important for me was to
make a non-hierarchal proposal, by taking the
exciting risk of flirting with this big "load of
nonsense."

DB – You've taken over the Manoir in its entirety,
including the corridors and staircases. Is there
a beginning to the exhibition?

BL – It begins on the ground floor with two pho-
tographs by Gianni Motti, by way of a prologue.
They show him working for other artists, busy
realizing and installing their works in museums.
These images were taken at his request by
the artists, in the present case Karen Kilimnik
and Rosemarie Trockel. I chose them in order to
instill a certain doubt with regard to the other
works in the exhibition and the expectation that
we may have in relation to artistic work, as well
as to test received ideas about this process.
Moreover, these questions, evoked with much

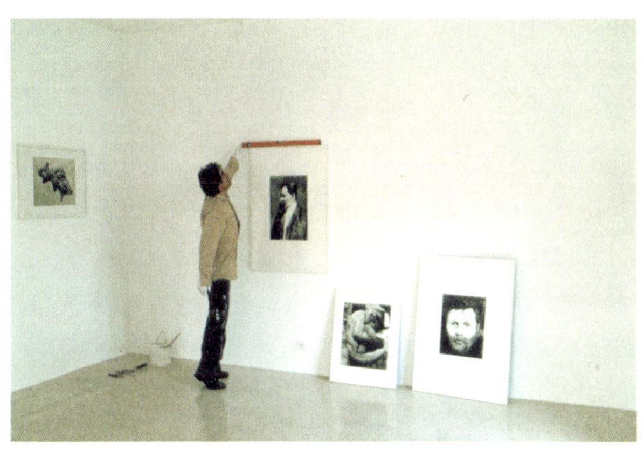

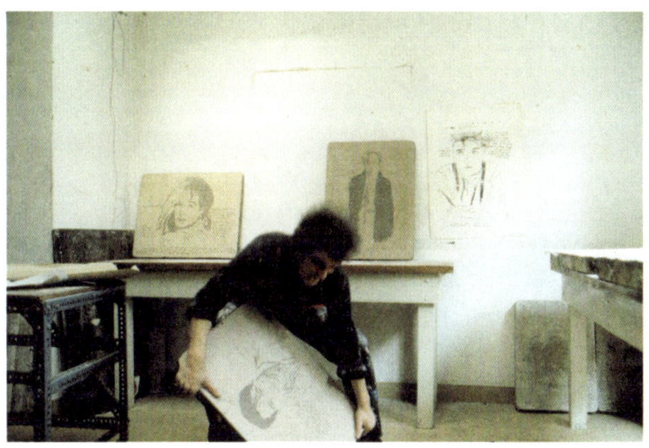

Gianni Motti
Untitled (Rosemarie Trockel), "Cushy Job" series, 1996
Tiger (Karen Kilimnik), "Cushy Job" series, 1995

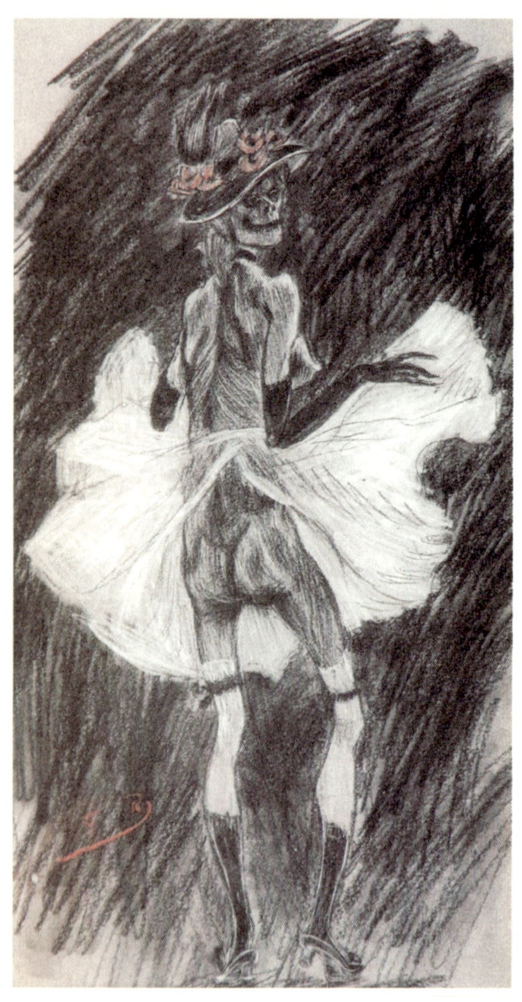

Félicien Rops, *La Mort qui danse*, 1865

humor by Gianni Motti, are woven through the entire exhibition.

DB — After this prologue, which signals a certain distance by playing with the relationship between the artist, the commissioner, and the "executer," the exhibition radically changes tone. It appears to leave Conceptual art behind with this wall in the stairwell, which is covered by 18 very different works.

BL — Another point of departure was the Ville de Martigny's Collection, where I found, among other things, an original engraving by Félicien Rops (1833–1898) in the garret dust! I therefore began a game of dominoes based on this Collection and its many works evoking the official history of the region. It was a filter that urged me to search for local anti-establishment art, for example. I titled this wall "Fantastic Paraphrenia," from the name of the psychiatric disorder, the sufferers of which construct a hallucinatory world, while always remaining connected to reality. The story thus begins with Oscar Darbellay (1903–1985), a native of Valais, and his photograph showing the flooding of Martigny in 1948. Then comes the romantic old engraving of a destroyed village and two contemporary drawings: *Kali-Yuga* (2009) by Vidya

Gastaldon—the dark age preceding the Buddhist revival—and one by Kim Seob Boninsegni (*Confusion*, 2009) in which we find, between other codified elements, the motif of chaos as it is represented in the Tarot. The fifth work is an original drawing for a Samael album cover. This Black Metal band comes from the region and is internationally renowned. Altogether, these works produce an apocalyptic story.

DB – An apocalyptic story that develops through analogies and echoes.

BL – This is the only place where I've really manipulated the images in favor of fiction. The analogy can obviously transform into a Pandora's Box: everything can go into it, everything functions. It must exclusively serve to broaden our vision and not the contrary. It must therefore not remain open for too long.

DB – It was Harald Szeemann who reintroduced this kind of cabinet of curiosities as a possible alternative to great narratives, which turned out to be a liberating gesture. As did, for that matter, during the same period of the 1970s, Daniel Spoerri and Marie-Louise Plessen with their *Musée sentimental*, organized in very different contexts.

BL – Indeed, but Szeemann's method has its limits. It subjected too many works to his curator's subjectivity. Personally, I am more interested in Serge Diaghilev's exhibition and magazine *Mir Iskusstva*, or Alexandre Dorner's work in Hannover. Today some interesting models are the rather anarchic ones of the art fair or the very subjective ones of the private collection. The reading of either of these resists all theory. As for the cabinet of curiosities, it is not standard practice. This way of seeing the world, the analogical mode of thinking, disappeared with the Enlightenment and only reappeared now and again, with Surrealism, for example, or as you say with Spoerri or Szeemann in a Fluxus sensibility. Today I feel that the contemporary scene has very much withdrawn into itself. Art is obsessed with "culture." Jeff Rian speaks of culture as "art's favorite pet." We quote, remix, and dissect it, but we're extremely timid when it comes to truly confronting it.

DB – How did you compose the rest of this wall?

BL – On the "Fantastic Paraphrenia" wall, after natural destruction and images of chaos, comes political threat, with caricatures of local politicians. There is a page from the *Le Crétin des Alpes* journal—along with the weekly *La Pilule*

(1970–1975), *Le Crétin* was one of the two single anarchist reviews of French-speaking Switzerland, edited in 1979 by the Valais writer and free-thinker Narcisse Praz (born in 1929). The page shows Hitler reading this publication and, alongside it, there is a drawing from a Martigny punk fanzine published in the 1980s, with a caricature of Rembart, the politician who invited French National Front leader Jean-Marie Le Pen to Martigny. The fanzine's logo is an allusion to *Le Nouvelliste*, a daily that was run until a few years ago by an extreme right religious conglomerate from Valais, linked to the famous Lefebvrists excommunicated by the Pope in 1978. Lastly, there is another drawing created for a T-shirt for Samael, and anarcho-syndicalist engravings of Geneva in the 1920s. The whole recounts an apocalypse, a political paraphrenia.

DB — There is also the element made of iron inserted between different frames.

BL — That's *Le Bouche-Trou*, a facetious work by François Morellet. Collectors complained that they no longer had any space on their walls as an excuse for no longer buying art, so he made them a *bouche-trou* (literally a "hole filler"), a "stopgap" to put between paintings.

DB – You establish analogies of a formal or content-based kind that allow you to connect elements that are usually heterogeneous. How does the third block on this wall function, the cards and views of landscapes that you associate with faces, in particular a *Distorted Face* by Jim Shaw?

BL – Cartography and portrait, the arbitrary remodeling of landscape, the portrait as illusion of objectivity …

DB – A thing that's impossible without abstraction if we wish at the same time to keep an image unique and recognizable.

BL – This section of the exhibition is like a seedling, an exhibition that remains to be done.

DB – It would be necessary to add Chuck Close …

BL – And works by Joe Coleman, which we couldn't get hold of in the end for logistical reasons.
Let's go up to the next floor, with three works in repoussé copper by the French-Swiss artist Bertram Schoch (b. 1906) in the corridor at the top of the stairs. This creator of "art brut" is unfortunately now forgotten. His works are hung not far from a painting by Josh Smith

and a watercolor by David Shrigley, brought in spontaneously by Valentin Carron not long before the opening.

DB — We then go into the first room that has the atmosphere of a "real" exhibition room, with these famous Lötschental masks, so-called "popular" art artifacts, and the *Histoire naturelle (Natural History)* lithographic series by Max Ernst from 1926.

BL — Here it's the creative process, the relationship between the contingency and the creation of a work that is questioned. These masks are peculiar in the sense that they are not entirely sculpted, but realized with bits of found wood, with an anthropomorphic appearance. They are then transformed by the sculptor, with few interventions, into frightening masks. Max Ernst's "frottages" function in a relatively similar manner. This is the kind of dialogue that I try to bring forth. The phantasmagorical then continues in the following room with the drawings by the Syro-Swiss artist Hayan Kam Nakache, which I've put opposite erotic engravings by Achille Chappaz, an artist from the region who is now in his 60s, and who is virtually unknown. It was he who told me about the work of Rodolphe Bresdin, a 19th-century French artist and Odilon

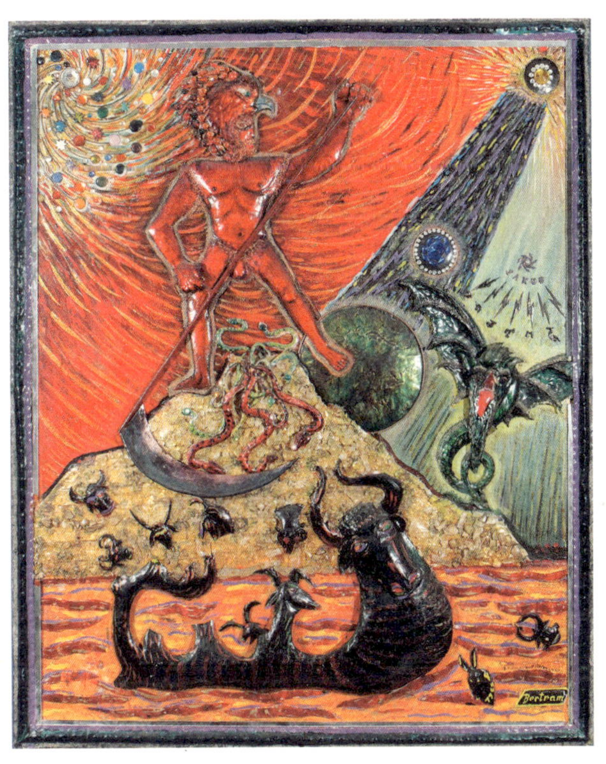

Bertram Schoch, *Le Héros solaire*, c. 1968

Redon's technical and spiritual master, who features in the large staircase on the second floor. The room's third element is a painting by Mamie Holst, *Landscape Before Dying*.

DB – After this primitive, erotic, and frightening imagery, why then pass into the void with, in the following room, a simple chalk circle by Ian Wilson? Are fantasies afraid of empty space? The void as means to escape fantasies? In fact, it's a kind of "Landscape Before Dying."

BL – Ah hah! Yes, a "landscape before the death of retinal art" ... Therefore, after these obsessive micro-worlds, we enter a room that presents the last "physical" work by Ian Wilson, realized in 1968—before he went on to only organize "conversations." It is a white circle with a one-meter radius traced on the floor with chalk. It's an iconoclastic moment of pause that leads us directly to the following situation: four works, four artists who express a position of doubt with regard to the principle of image production and who question the validity of stories in which images are inserted: Guyton\Walker, Alex Hubbard, Steven Parrino, and this recumbent Christ from the Haut-Valais. The artists express their defiance toward the image, while nevertheless still creating objects. There is no aniconism here, but an ambiguous position, on the razor's edge.

DB – Isn't this Christ in fact an icon, though?

BL – Yes and no, to be precise. It was made in the 14th century, a period when theologians rethought Christian spirituality and carried out a "little revolution" before the great Reformation of the 15th and 16th centuries. As the faithful were more inclined to pray to the image or idol of Christ, repugnant representations of Christ were created so that the faithful would be conscious that one must not adore an image, but a "beyond the image." The sculptor has exaggerated the morbid character of this Christ, with a gaping thorax wound. The sculpture was polychrome and streaked with representations of blood—we can see traces here and there. It was sanded during the Counter-Reformation, because it was considered too colorful and indeed too seductive. This object testifies to two successive attempts to put the image's power of seduction at a distance. In fact, our gaze changes constantly: we read an object, an image, differently according to the context.

DB – That's true for many artists, what's more it works both ways: for admiration as well as for rejection, from William Bouguereau, El Greco, and Bernard Buffet to Francis Picabia and Louise Bourgeois. The reception of their work seems to strongly depend on the context, while we tend to admire a sculpture by Constantin Brancusi for its autonomy, for its form and its "intrinsic" and almost timeless qualities. An artist like Richard Serra tries to be conscious of a precise context and seems at the same time driven by the ambition to realize an absolute and perfect form, which obviously pleases the market as much as it does art historians.

BL – Once again, I wanted to propose specific situations, to see what happens when these objects are gathered together and interact. It's for these reasons that I also wanted to show the paintings by Bertram Schoch and the *Tachistisches Kleisterbild* by H.R. Giger from 1964. I wanted there to be a possible reinterpretation stemming from the works themselves, therefore beyond the established narratives, which to me don't explain the simultaneous coexistence of antagonist productions. I think that we have a kind of duty to reread history and stories, and to see what has been left out.

DB – It's a pleasure to do so.

BL — Absolutely, I totally accept all these works, without cynicism. I simply want to focus the fact that there are 10 or 15 *stories* being written at the same time. And each person can have a subjective reading of them. Just as I find that we live in a very mannered period, both conceptually and formally. And these works from the past come and tap us on the shoulder to remind us that nothing can ever be counted on!

DB — In this exhibition, we go from the image of the Apocalypse and political, natural, and esoteric threat, to doubting representation, passing by the production of the image linked to contingency and the phantasmagorical. We then find ourselves in front of a "non-image," only to finish by flirting, when confronted with the enamels by Bertram Schoch, with a kind of total affirmation of the image as space of seduction. But the exhibition doesn't stop there. You add a chapter on the question of the mental image, which unfolds in the staircase that climbs to the second floor and which brings together works by Andreas Dobler, Josse Bailly, Hans Bellmer, Marta Riniker-Radich, R.M. Ramagli, Cédric Eisenring, H.R. Giger, Robert Morris, Louis Soutter, Julien Carreyn, Vidya Gastaldon, Marguerite Burnat-Provins, Rodolphe Bresdin, Emanuel Rossetti, Olivier Taramarcaz, Mamie

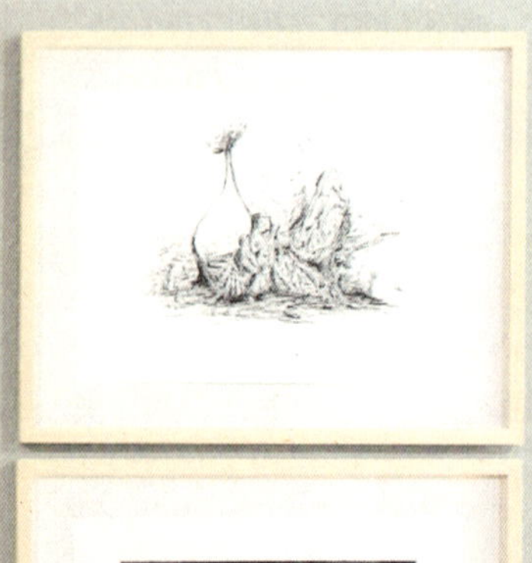

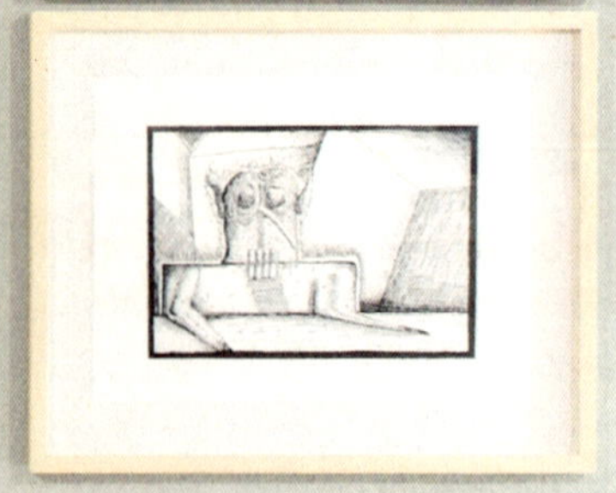

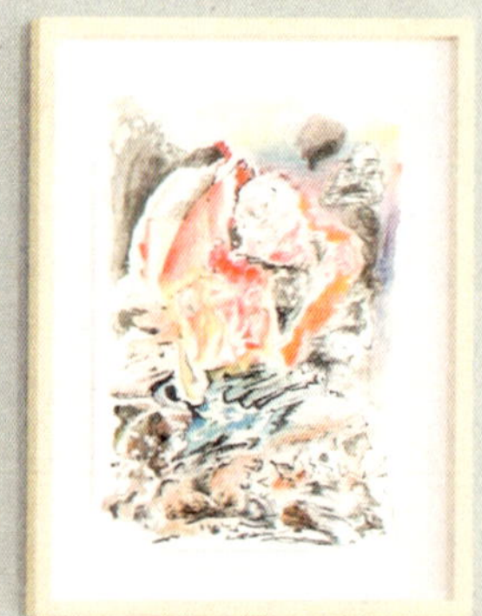

Hayan Kam Nakache, drawings, 2010–2011

Holst and others, artists known and unknown, and from very different periods.

BL – Yes, there was even a museum technician who came one morning with an engraving by his cousin, which we have integrated into this group, once again mounted in the style of an amateur's cabinet. It's a kind of drifting through heterogeneous mental spaces that, at the top of the staircase, continues with the works by the Haitian artist Préfète Duffaut, the visionary artist Norbert H. Kox, a drawing by Elvis Studio and a video documenting a performance by Michael Kimber, in which a character finds himself in a claustrophobic situation that he literally tries to unravel. The notion of "mental space" is an interesting filter. It is comprehensible enough for the visitor not to become lost, and yet vague enough to allow a free and subjective progression. It's the link between precise and hazy that is interesting.

DB – Then comes a situation that is almost opposite or "technical," that of the mechanism of distribution and the multiplied accessibility of images, in a room bringing together Seth Price, Valentin Carron, and 17th-century works by Abraham Bosse that depict the mass production of engravings at printing workshops. During the

17th century, engraving workshops were behind the circulation of images and established models of composition, hierarchies, and values. It was a real system of image distribution that was supplanted by the development of lithograph printing, then later by offset printing, and today by the Internet. We could assert: who says distribution says value, because it is distribution that assures presence and this is often taken for a sign of importance, of value.

BL — It is actually one of the filters that helped me install this room. There are obviously many other readings possible. On the Internet, Seth Price found JPG images of wall paintings taken from the copy of the Lascaux Cave. He reprinted them on Mylar, and then duplicated them arbitrarily. He isolated a cultural sign in the same way that Valentin Carron isolates a precise cultural element, in this case a detail of local architecture that he renders monumentally.

DB — Both remove an element from one context to then immediately reinject it into another. In this room, as in the one with the Christ, you introduce a kind of mass distribution image, shared and appreciated *en masse*, in contrast to images of a phantasmagorical kind, very linked to an individual, to hallucinogenic trips, to

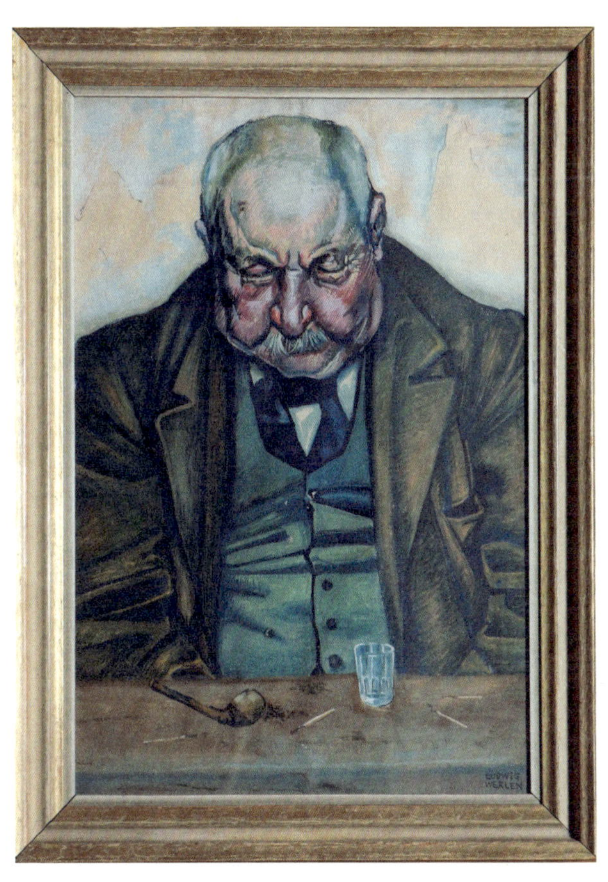

Ludwig Werlen, *Le Buveur ou un verre de trop*, 1922

personal pleasures, and to the images' ability to evoke the latter. At the same time, we realize that these phantasmagorical images depend just as much on established models and wide-spread conventions, which is moreover what Surrealism proved by very quickly becoming a boring thing. That said, art history believes that with Surrealism we had considered the phantasmagorical image from all angles, that it had been put away once and for all, domesticated.

BL – Exactly. Genres merge and mass distributed images become those that condition the personal fantasies that you were talking about, and vice versa. Hence the necessity for artists to transgress what becomes the norm. We are now in the Manoir's large ceremonial room, where the building's first owner's will for *grandeur* is best expressed. Here I've installed types of vanities. On the wall there is the *Le Buveur ou un verre de trop* (*The Drinker or One Glass Too Many*, 1922) by Ludwig Werlen (1884–1928), a painter from the Haut-Valais, which depicts an aristocrat alone, asleep in a café, and resting on his laurels. At the other end of the room I've placed *La Mort qui danse* (1865) by Félicien Rops. In the center of the room, two works speak of art as an object of social prestige: a painting by Tobias Madison, art for an intercontinental company lounge. On the other side is a trompe-l'œil canvas by Domenico Rabiato realized in 1766 for an interior decor of the Château de Courten in Sierre. It was commissioned by an officer from Valais, Eugène de Courten, a mercenary who, upon his return to Valais, commissioned artists and craftsmen to imitate the style of the French aristocratic residences he'd seen during his travels.

DB – And why finish the exhibition with abstract art and the works of Stéphane Dafflon, Francis Baudevin, Mirza Zwissig, and Blaise Coutaz? Is it a question of concluding with phantom images?

BL – The works by Baudevin and Coutaz could indeed be seen as phantom images because both have a mnemonic character, one in an autobiographical style, the other calling on our collective memory. As Dafflon's painting is slightly Op, we could digress on the visual effect created in the brain of the onlooker ... This painting is literally a black hole devouring space, its presence in the room has visually swallowed all the other objects that were there when the exhibition's installation began. This is why, as it was important to respect the objects without imposing a reading theoretically defined in advance, there are only two works here. We are completely

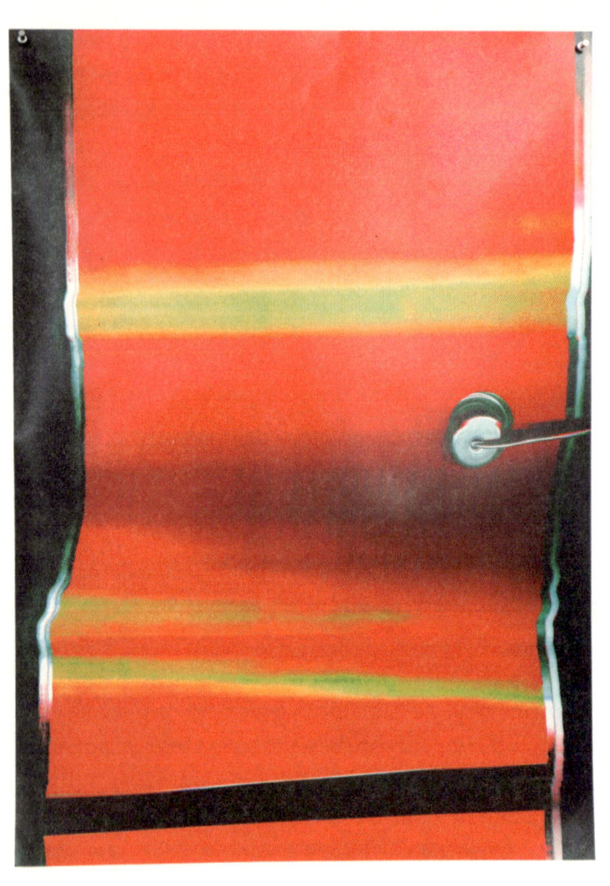

Guyton\Walker, *Christmas Poster*, 2010

immersed in spatial questions. In the case of Baudevin's work—the wallpaper lining the corridor—we are at a point of friction between abstract painting, decoration, figuration (the motif quotes the flyleaves of *Tintin* albums), and most particularly the conceptual gesture. The wallpaper delimits a specific space in the building. As for Zwissig (1942–1995), she is one of the rare representatives of geometrical abstraction in Valais, at a time when lyrical abstraction was dominant. I'm actually not sure that the exhibition ends with this group. On the one hand, the corridor covered with *Moulinsart* by Baudevin and the work by Coutaz rejoin the "mental space" zone and, on the other hand, just after Dafflon's painting and Zwissig's two adhesives, there is a small, discreet staircase that, if we choose to take it, leads us to the first floor and to the works by Guyton\Walker and Steven Parrino.

DB – This exhibition thinks with and through the images and lets itself be guided by what they evoke, say, and represent. It doesn't offer pretentious theory, but another gaze; it brings together disparate works and moves forward by associations and connections. It has us lean out the window in order to see further into the distance. It makes total sense to me; it's like a stroll that by turns leaves me lost, surprised, and inspired. All the people I know have appreciated its sensitivity, humor, and strangeness. At the same time, it remains powerless, in the sense that it will not change hierarchies or great narratives. It is a magnificent "Don Quichottery," isn't that right?

BL – A suggestive, fanciful, and self-sufficient vision of art would correspond to a parallel world built by a visionary. I am very divided over your metaphor, flattered and at the same time uncomfortable. I think that individuals can read this exhibition without any problem, indeed it was meant to be read and reread, to be questionned, through the onlooker's subjectivity. On the other hand, maybe the institution cannot or perhap will not lend itself to this exercise. I wonder frankly if the White Cube ideal, aspiring to isolate works from the world, is not a far more fanciful model than the one proposed by this exhibition. On the condition that the world from which we describe it is not itself an illusion …

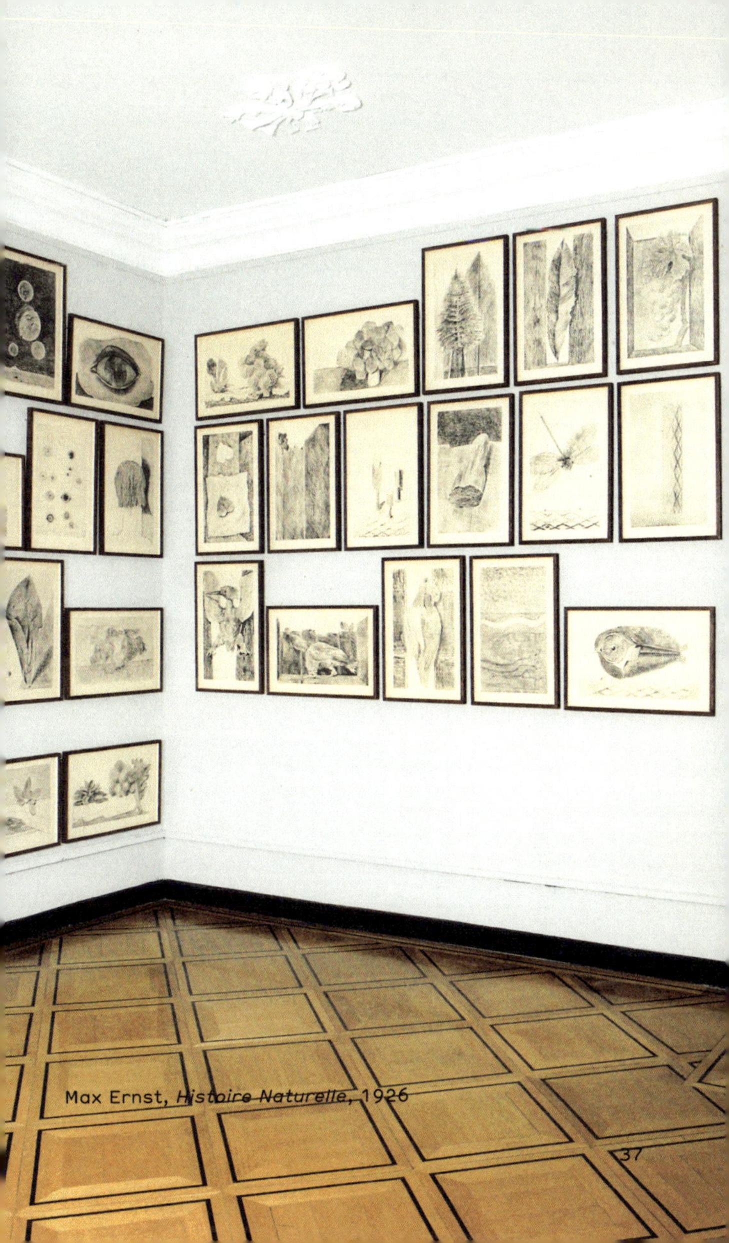

Max Ernst, *Histoire Naturelle*, 1926

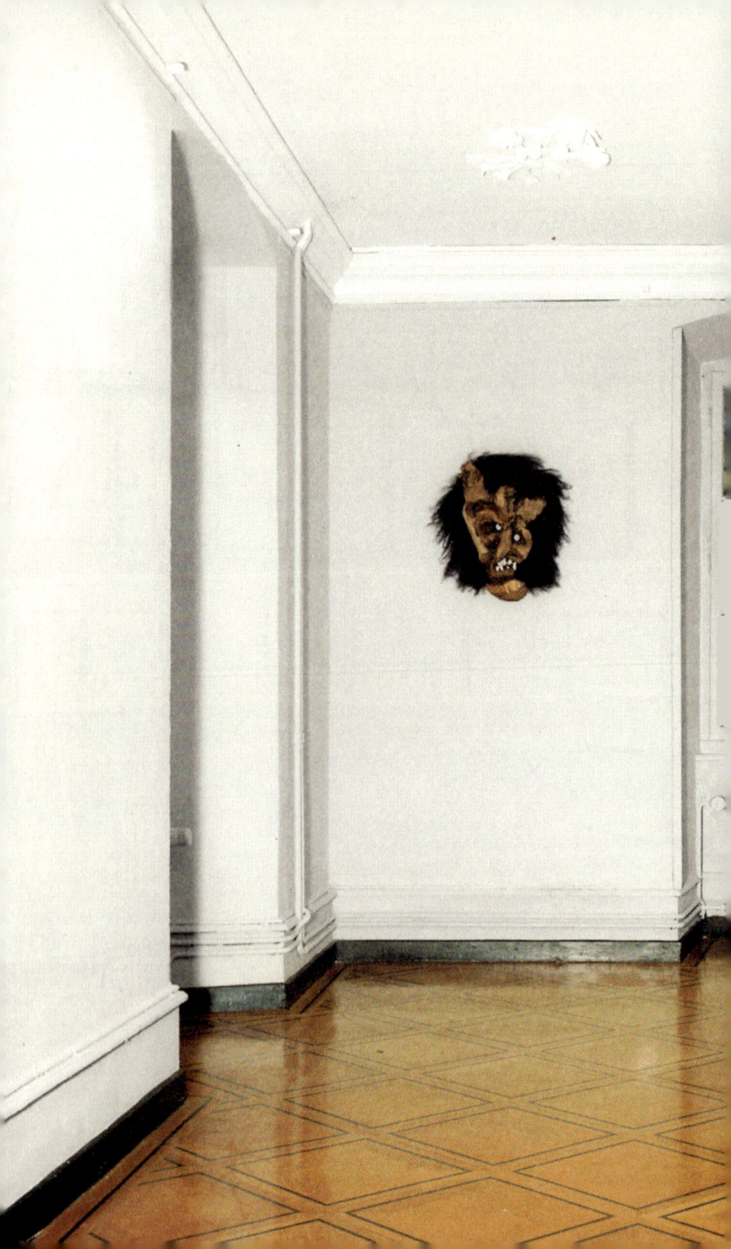

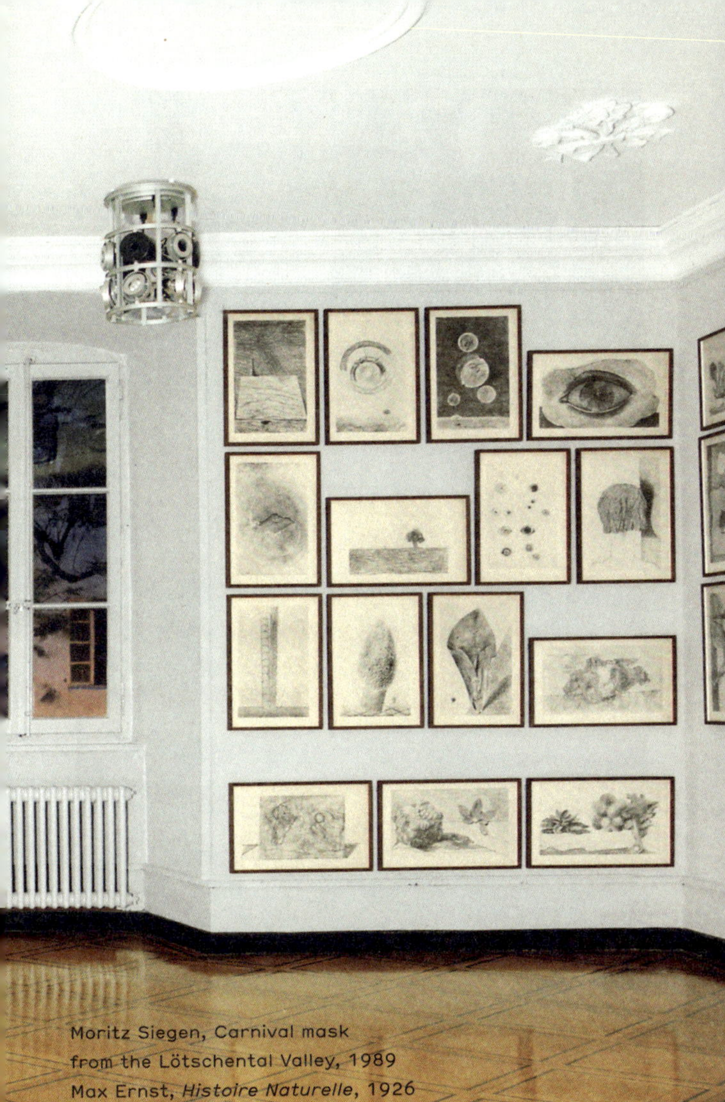

Moritz Siegen, Carnival mask
from the Lötschental Valley, 1989
Max Ernst, *Histoire Naturelle*, 1926

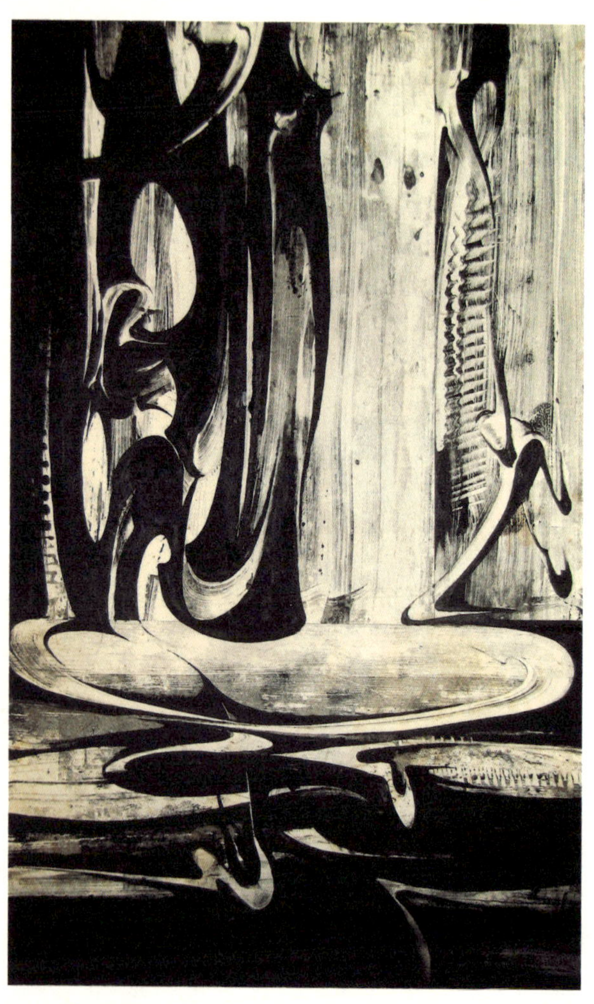

H.R. Giger, *Tachistisches Kleisterbild*, 1964

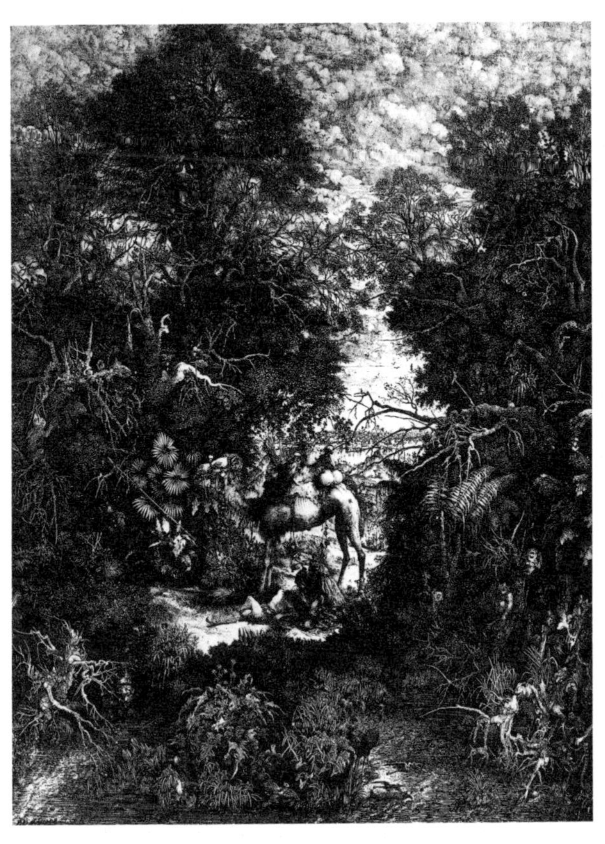

Rodolphe Bresdin, *Le Bon Samaritain*, 1861
Exhibition views, "Mental Landscape" section →

41

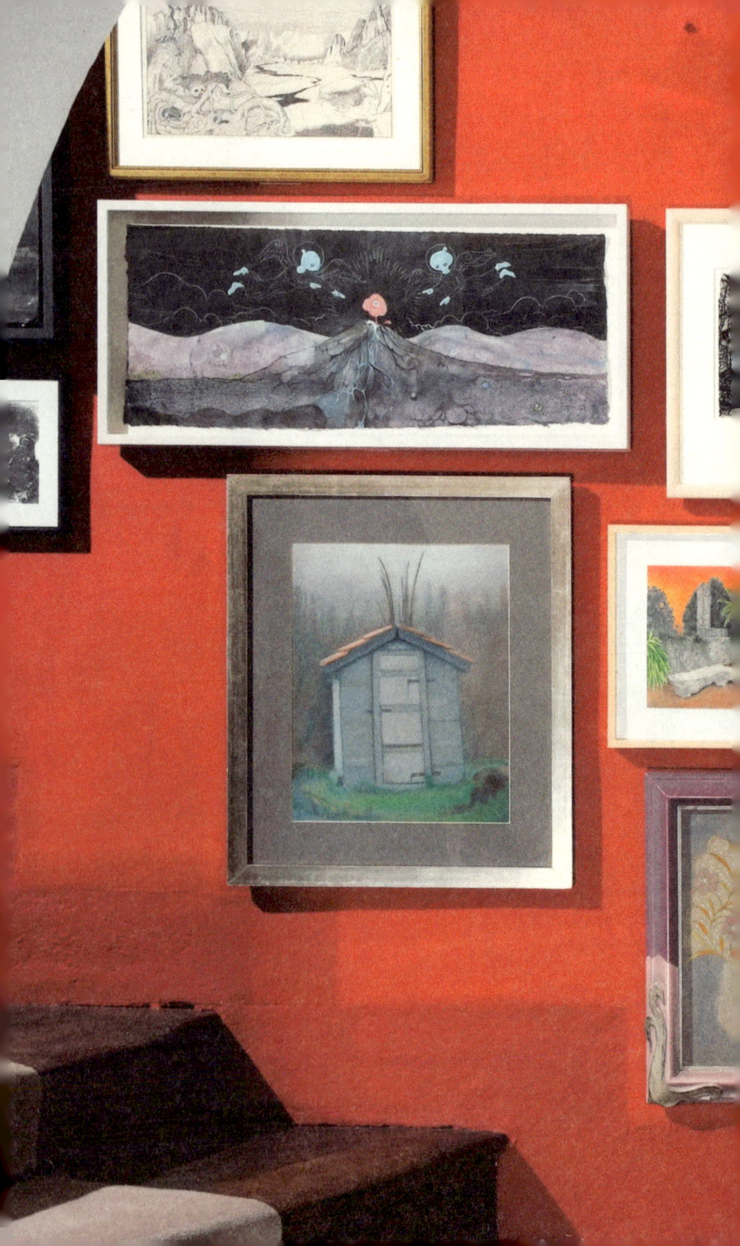

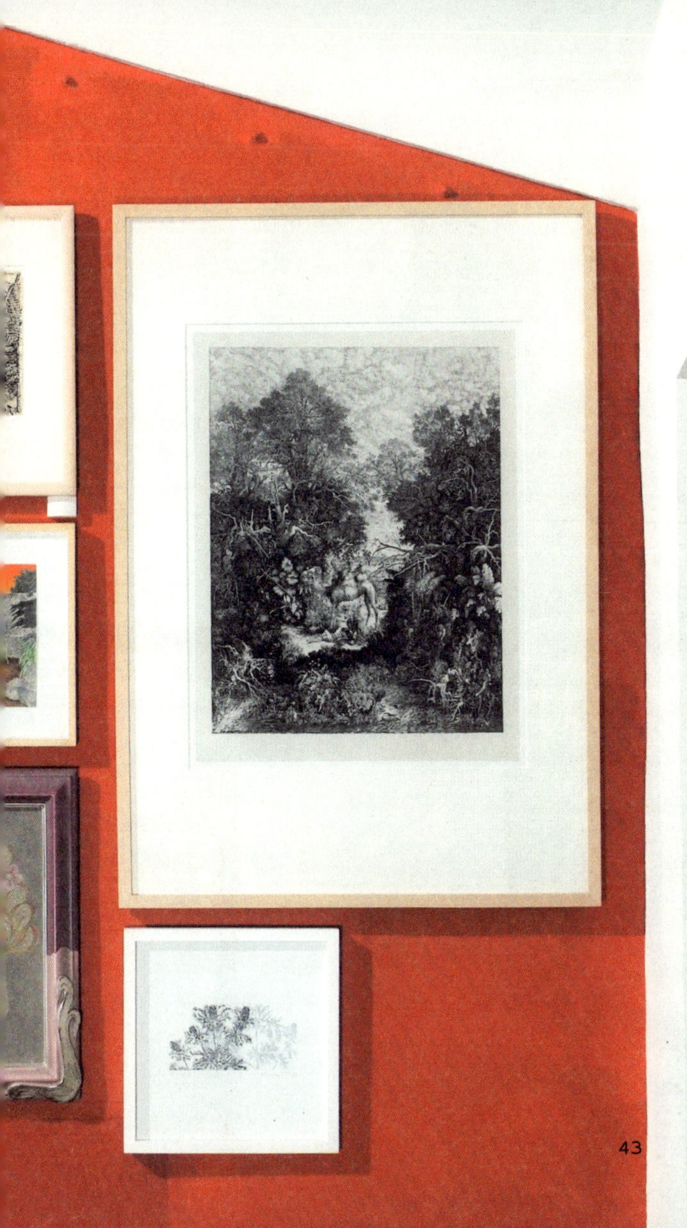

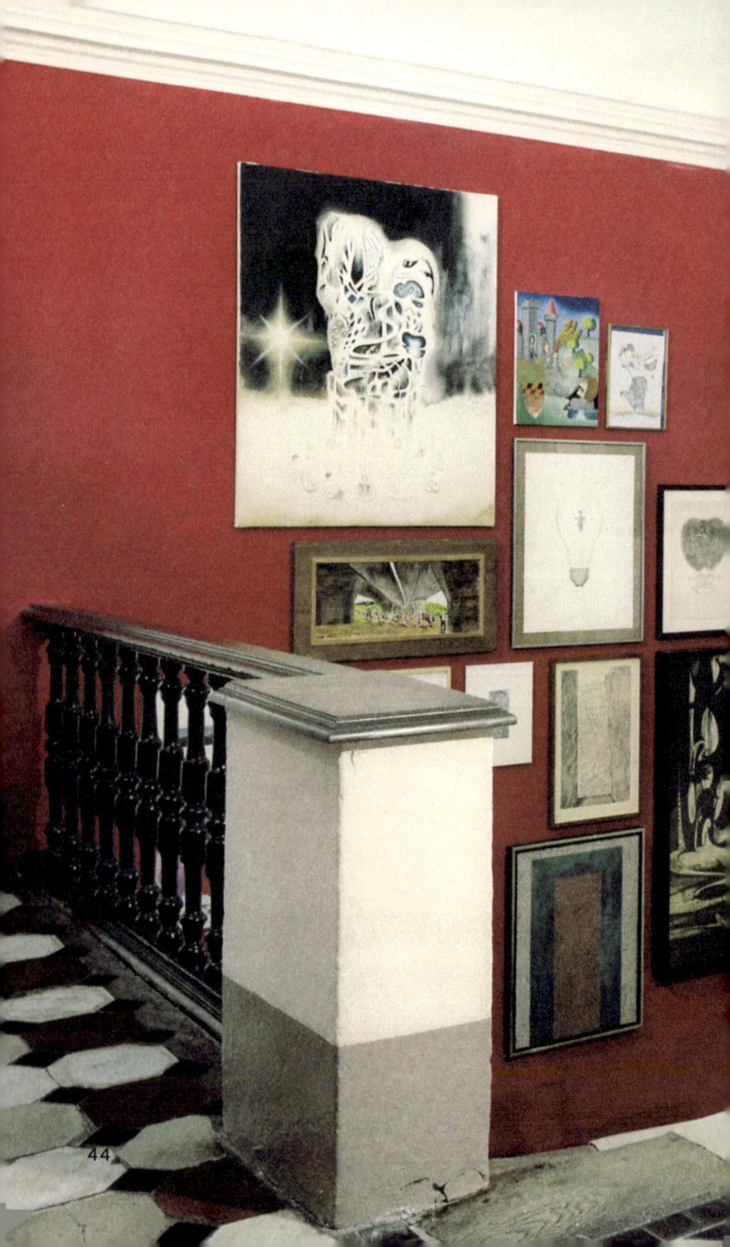

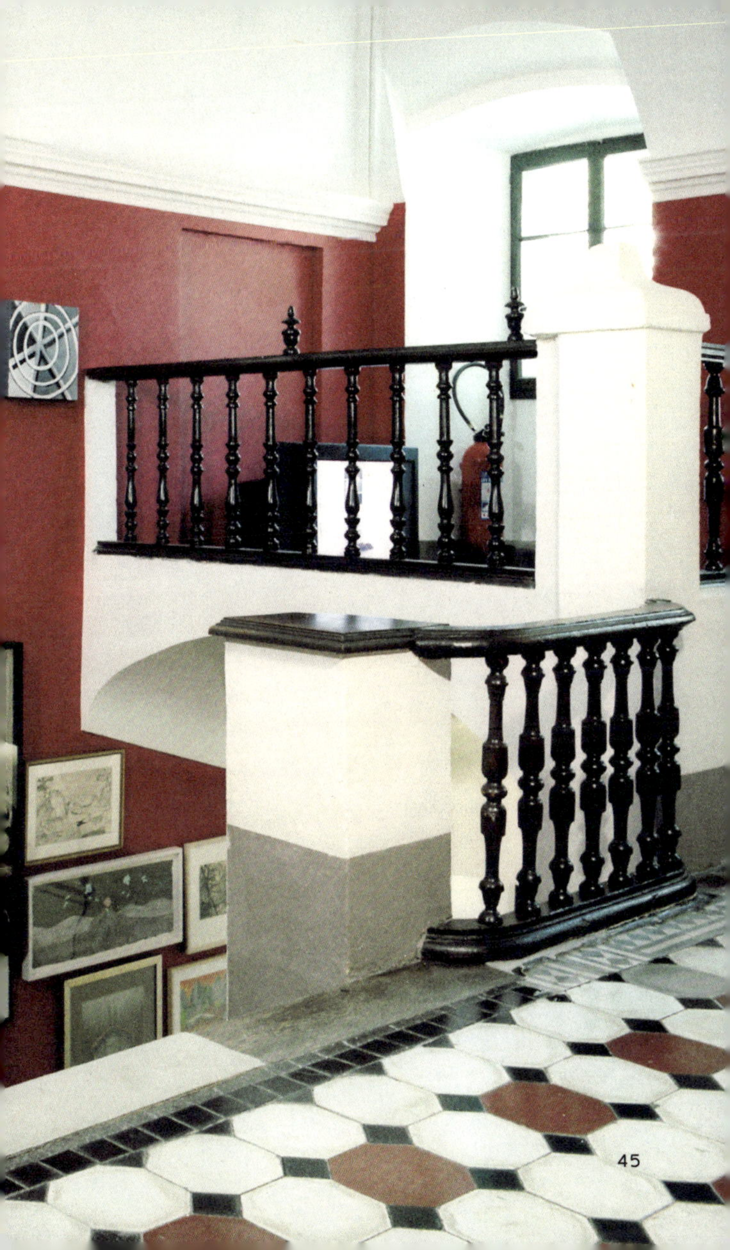

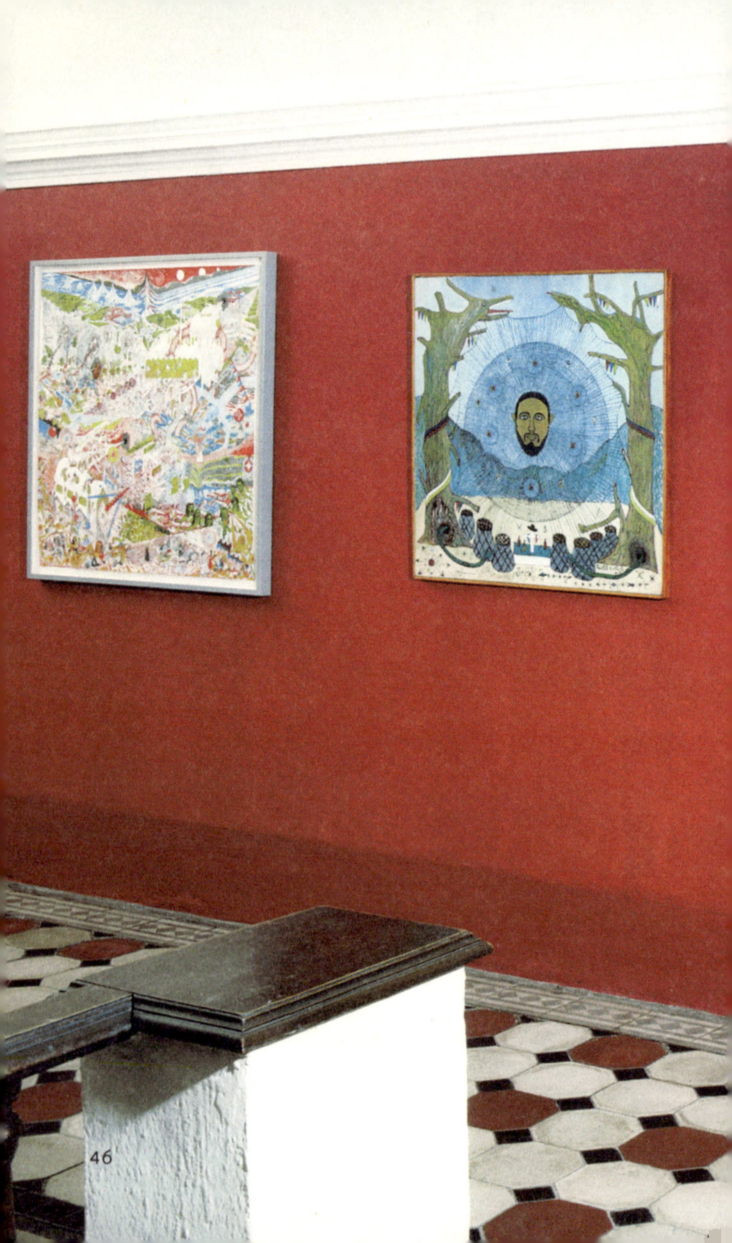

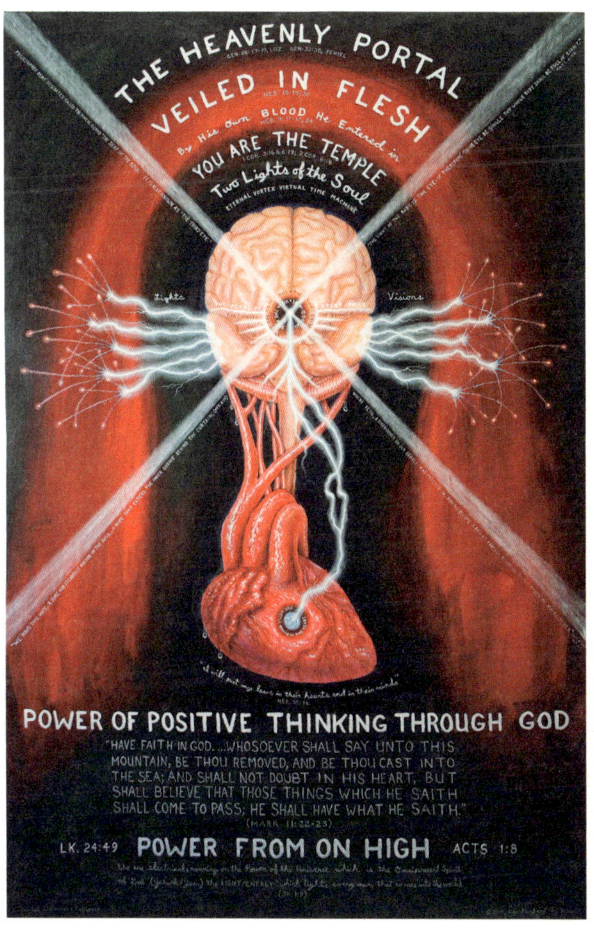

Norbert H. Kox, *Brain Heart*, 2011

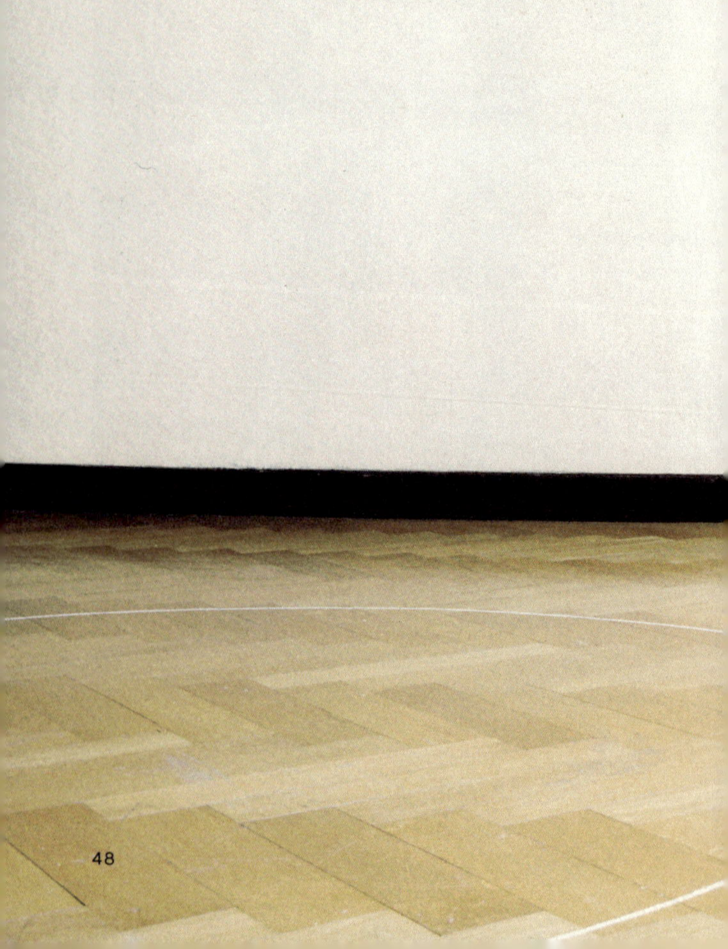

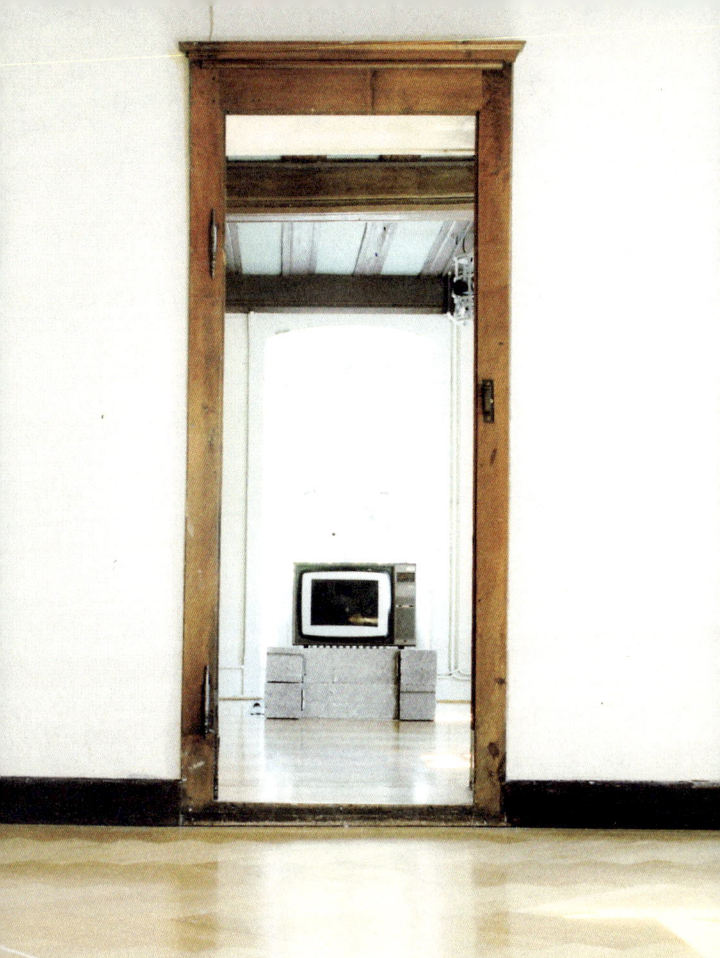

Ian Wilson, *The 10th Circle on the Floor*, 1968
Steven Parrino, *Untitled*, 1982–2002

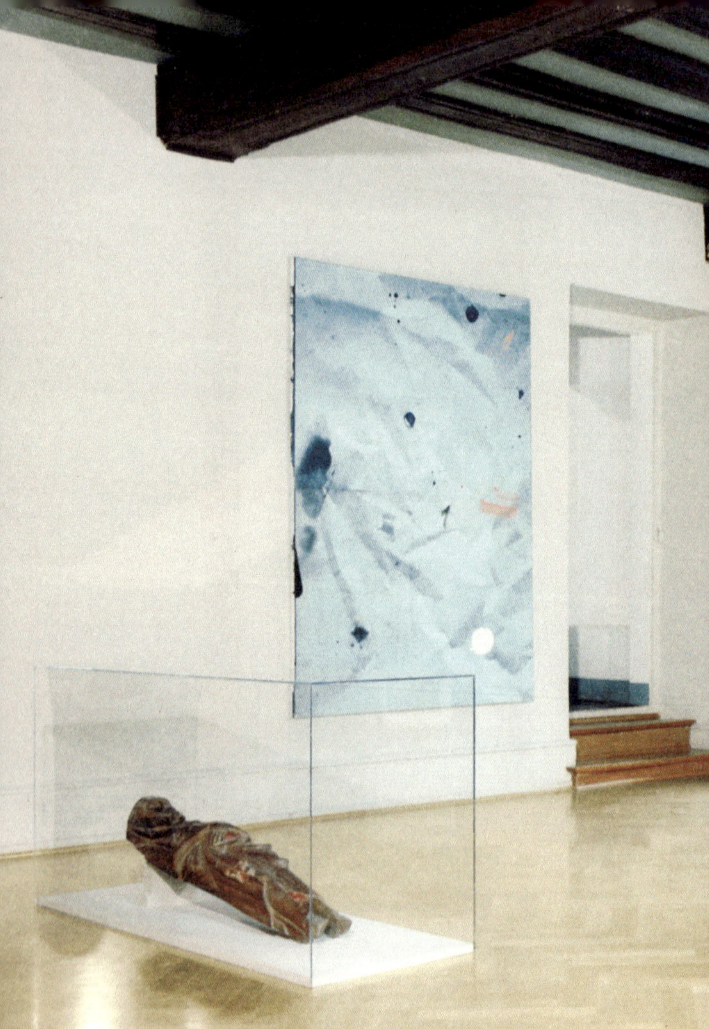

Reclining Christ from the Haut-Valais, mid-14th century
Alex Hubbard, *Untitled (SOP4)*, 2008
Steven Parrino, *Untitled*, 1982–2002

50

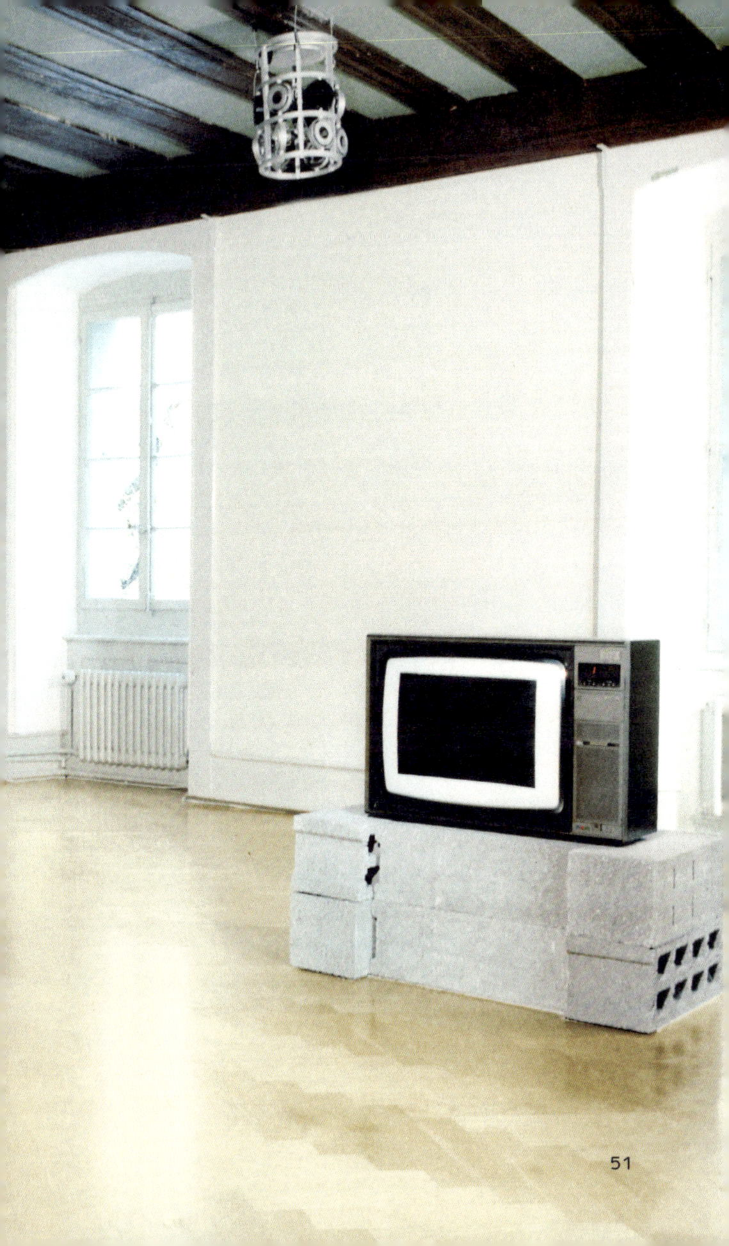

List of Works

The list of works includes all works presented in the exhibition *Adventures, Reflections, and Ambushes*. They are not all reproduced in this publication.

Anonymous
Reclining Christ from the
Haut-Valais, mid-14th century
Wood, 107 × 23 × 18 cm
Collection Musée Cantonal
d'Histoire du Valais, Sion

Anonymous
Le Crétin des Alpes, 1979
India ink on paper, 35 × 29.8 cm
Collection Narcisse Praz

Anonymous
Menu du Conseil communal à l'Hôtel Kluster & Poste, 1911
Lithograph, 21 × 27 cm
Collection Ville de Martigny

Anonymous
Village détruit, Ottonelle, c. 1850
Etching, 39 × 44.5 cm
Collection Ville de Martigny

Anonymous
Napoléon Bonaparte au Grand-Saint-Bernard, c. 1802
Etching and letter framed,
58 × 102 cm
Collection Ville de Martigny

Anonymous
Geographic map of the Duché
de Savoie, mid-19th century
35 × 33 cm
Collection Ville de Martigny

Josse Bailly
Kingdom Come, 2011
Oil paint on canvas, 40 × 30 cm
Courtesy Galerie Saks, Geneva

Francis Baudevin
Moulinsart, 2008
Wallpaper, dimensions variable
Courtesy Wallpapers by Artists,
Dijon

Hans Bellmer
Bottines, 1951
Lithograph, 38 × 28 cm
Collection Marco Witzig, Zurich

Jacques Berthet
Usine d'aluminium, n.d.
Photograph, 58.5 × 55 cm
Collection Ville de Martigny

A. Bessi
Untitled, c. 1995
Oil paint on canvas, 28 × 34 cm
Collection Ville de Martigny

Edmond Bille
Civilisation, "Une Danse macabre"
series, 1919

Mensonges, "Une Danse macabre"
series, 1919
Wood engravings, 24.5 × 17.5 cm

Collection Musée d'Art du Valais,
Sion

Kim Seob Boninsegni
Confusion, 2009
India ink on paper, 32 × 40 cm
Collection Mai-Thu Perret, Geneva

Abraham Bosse
Les Graveurs en taille-douce, 1643
Etching, 26 × 32.6 cm
Collection Etat de Vaud, Musée
Jenisch, Vevey, Cabinet cantonal
des estampes

Les Imprimeurs en taille-douce,
1642
Etching, 26 × 32.6 cm
Collection Etat de Vaud, Musée
Jenisch, Vevey, Cabinet cantonal
des estampes

Michel Bovisi
La Porte, 2010
Oil paint and grease crayon
on canvas, 60 × 40 cm
Collection of the artist

Rodolphe Bresdin
Le Bon Samaritain, 1861
Lithograph, 90 × 63.4 cm
Collection Etat de Vaud, Musée
Jenisch, Vevey, Cabinet cantonal
des estampes

Marguerite Burnat-Provins
Ma Ville – Amulrène, 1950
Pastel and watercolor on paper,
35 × 24.5 cm
Private collection

Julien Carreyn
Crysel, 2010
Laserprint paper, 11.5 × 4 cm
Courtesy Galerie Crèvecoeur, Paris

Valentin Carron
Untitled, 2004
Polystyrene, fiberglass, acrylic
resin, acrylic paint,
118 × 101 × 105 cm
Collection Christian & Thérèse
Cuenoud, Geneva

Achille Chappaz
Les Diables, 2010
Lithograph, 40 × 30 cm
Edition of 50 copies
Collection Balthazar Lovay

Achille Chappaz
Les Jets et les batons, 2008
Lithograph, 40 × 24 cm
Edition of 50 copies
Collection of the artist

Progéniture(s), 2007
Lithograph, 40 × 30 cm
Edition of 50 copies
Collection of the artist

Blaise Coutaz
Chalet, 2010
Wood paneling, 75 × 107 cm
Collection of the artist

Stéphane Dafflon
AST132, 2009
Acrylic on canvas, 191 × 191 cm
Collection of the artist
Photo: Ilmari Kalkkinen/MAMCO,
Geneva

Oscar Darbellay
Inondation de 1948, 1948
Photograph, 43 × 50 cm
Collection Ville de Martigny

Andreas Dobler
Der Wille zum Design, 2010
Acrylic on canvas, 98 × 80 cm
Collection Mai-Thu Perret, Geneva

Préfète Duffaut
La Toile d'araignée, 2004
Oil paint on canvas, 75 × 75 cm
Collection Nathalie Rebholz,
Geneva

Cédric Eisenring
Untitled, 2010
Inkjet print on paper, 21 × 30 cm
Collection of the artist

Max Ernst
Histoire Naturelle, 1926
Portfolio of 34 collotypes on Japan
Imperial paper, 50 × 32.5 cm
Private collection, Geneva

Vidya Gastaldon
Entraterrestre, 2009
Acrylic, watercolor, color pencil
on paper, 29 × 72.7 cm
Courtesy Galerie Guy Bärtschi,
Geneva

Kali-Yuga, 2009
Acrylic, watercolor, color pencil
on paper, 29 × 38 cm
Courtesy Galerie Guy Bärtschi,
Geneva

Alberto Giacometti
Mère de l'artiste assise II, 1964
Lithograph, 65 × 48 cm
Private collection

H.R. Giger
Tachistisches Kleisterbild, 1964
India ink on paper, 100 × 62 cm
Collection Marco Witzig, Zurich

Marie-Antoinette Gorret
Ampoule, 1982
Color pencil on paper, 64 × 50 cm
Collection Ville de Martigny

Michel Grillet
Montagnes-Ciel, 2005–2006
Watercolor on paper, 5.1 × 26 cm
Collection Musée d'Art du Valais,
Sion

Guyton\Walker
Christmas Poster, 2010
Offset print, 60 × 80 cm
Collection Balthazar Lovay

Mamie Holst
*Landscape Before Dying
(Circumstance)*, 2000
Acrylic on canvas, 33 × 33 cm
Private collection, Geneva

*Landscape Before Dying
(Voyage#2)*, 2000
Acrylic on canvas, 41 × 31 cm
Private collection, Geneva

Alex Hubbard
Untitled (SOP4), 2008
Silkscreen print and oil paint on
canvas, 183 × 127 cm
Collection Stéphane Ribordy, Geneva

Hayan Kam Nakache
Ca va le bocal ?, 2011
India Ink on paper, 40 × 30 cm

Dépressif, 2010
India Ink on paper, 29.7 × 21 cm

Les Sous-bois du Valais, 2010
India Ink on paper, 29.7 × 21 cm

Merci Max, 2011
India Ink on paper, 29.7 × 21 cm

Rêve polymorphe, 2009
Felt-tip, color pencil, and pencil
on paper, 21.5 × 52 cm

Viens visiter mon cottage, 2011
India Ink on paper, 21 × 29.7 cm

Vomito, 2011
India Ink on paper, 29.7 × 21 cm

All drawings courtesy Hard Hat,
Geneva

Michael Kimber
Solo encordé, 2010
Video performance, 55'36
Collection of the artist

Norbert H. Kox
Brain Heart, 2011
Acrylic on canvas, 162.5 × 106.5 cm
Courtesy Toxic Gallery Luxembourg

Dominique Lang
Worship Him (Samael), 1990
Pencil on tracing paper, 41 × 29.4 cm
Collection Samael, Riddes

Pierre Loye
Guérite anthropomorphe, 1983
Pastel on paper, 60.5 × 52 cm
Collection Ville de Martigny

Tobias Madison
Yes I Can, 2010
Acrylic on flag on canvas, Plexiglas,
150 × 200 cm
Courtesy Galerie Karma
International, Zurich

François Morellet
Le Bouche-Trou, 1996
Aluminum, 80 × 80 × 2.5 cm
Collection Mamco, Geneva

Robert Morris
Telegram: The Rationed Years, 1998
Charcoal on paper, 15 × 20 cm
Special edition of *Telegram: The
Rationed Years*, JRP Editions, 1998

Gianni Motti
Untitled (Rosemarie Trockel),
"Cushy Job" series, 1996
Photograph on aluminum,
50 × 70 cm
Collection Fonds d'art
contemporain de la Ville de Genève

Tiger (Karen Kilimnik),
"Cushy Job" series, 1996
Photograph on aluminum,
50 × 70 cm
Collection Fonds d'art
contemporain de la Ville de Genève

Charles-Clos Olsommer
Paysage onirique, c. 1910
India ink on paper, 24 × 36 cm
Collection Musée d'Art du Valais,
Sion

Steven Parrino
Untitled, 1982–2002
Spray paint on television,
cement bricks, 50 × 45 × 70 cm
Collection Circuit, Lausanne

Seth Price
Double Hunt, 2007
Laserprint on Mylar, 124 × 60 cm
Collection Stéphane Ribordy,
Geneva

Punk
Portrait de Rembart, c. 1988
India ink on paper, 29.6 × 21 cm
Collection Lulu Jacquérioz, Ravoire

Joseph Domenico Rabiatow
Part of a decor from the Castel
Eugène De Courten, Sierre, 1766
Oil painting on canvas,
275 × 97.5 cm
Musée Cantonal d'Histoire du
Valais, Sion

Marta Riniker-Radich
Florida Table, 2008
Color pencil and pencil on paper,
21 × 29.7 cm

Untitled (Sunrise Lobby), 2009
Color pencil and pencil on paper,
21 × 29.7 cm

All drawings courtesy Hard Hat,
Geneva

R.M. Ramagli
Poya sous l'autoroute, 2009
Acrylic on wood panel, 21.5 × 52 cm
Collection Balthazar Lovay

Félicien Rops
La Mort qui danse, 1865
Etching, 55 × 37 cm
Collection Ville de Martigny

Emanuel Rossetti
Bubble Club, 2011
Epson Ultrachrome K3 on archival
matte paper in polyprophylene
sleeve, 29 × 42 cm

Untitled, 2011
Epson Ultrachrome K3 on archival
matte paper in polyprophylene
sleeve, 29 × 42 cm

All works Courtesy Karma
International, Zürich

Bertram Schoch
Jeune fille, 1976
Enamel, fabric, and copper on wood
panel, 50 × 70 cm
Collection Jean-Louis Roy, Geneva

Guillaume Tell, 1978
Enamel and mixed media on
repoussé copper, 175.5 × 124 cm
Collection Musée d'Art du Valais,
Sion

Le Héros solaire, c. 1968
Enamel and mixed media on
repoussé copper, 135.5 × 111.5 cm
Collection Musée d'Art du Valais,
Sion

Vierge, 1978
Enamel and mixed media on
repoussé copper, 90 × 70 cm
Collection Jean-Louis Roy, Geneva

Jim Shaw
*Untitled #50 (Distorted Faces
Series)*, 1984
Airbrush, graphite, and pencil
on paper, 35 × 27 cm
Collection Eric Bertrand, Geneva

David Shrigley
Untitled (Relax in Peace), 2010
Ink and acrylic on paper,
46.5 × 34 cm
Collection Valentin Carron,
Martigny

Moritz Siegen
Carnival mask from the Lötschental
Valley, 1989
Wood, 60 × 40 cm
Lötschental Museum, Kippel

Skyll
François Mitterrand à Martigny,
1989
India ink on paper, 21 × 29.7 cm
Collection Ville de Martigny

Louis Soutter
Le Valais et l'hôtel de la forêt,
1923/1930
India ink on paper, 21.5 × 16.8
Collection Musée d'Art du Valais,
Sion

Elvis Studio
Elvis 1Hz, 2009
Color pencil on paper, 84 × 84.5 cm
Courtesy Hard Hat, Geneva

Olivier Taramarcaz
Panicaut des Alpes (chardon bleu),
2011
Etching, 10 × 20 cm
Collection of the artist

Éric Vuille
Samael Light, 1997
India ink on cardboard, 21 × 34 cm
Collection Samael, Riddes

Ludwig Werlen
Le Buveur ou un verre de trop,
1922
Gouache on paper, 65.8 × 45 cm
Collection Musée d'Art du Valais,
Sion

Agnes Rieder Wiler
Carnival mask from the Lötschental
Valley, c. 1980
Wood, 85 × 40 × 15 cm
Lötschental Museum, Kippel

Ian Wilson
The 10th Circle on the Floor, 1968
Chalk, ø 200 cm
Collection Mamco, Geneva

Mirza Zwissig
OCO, 1973–1974
Stickers on paper, 69.5 × 49.6 cm
(two from a series of 4 plates)
Collection Musée d'Art du Valais,
Sion

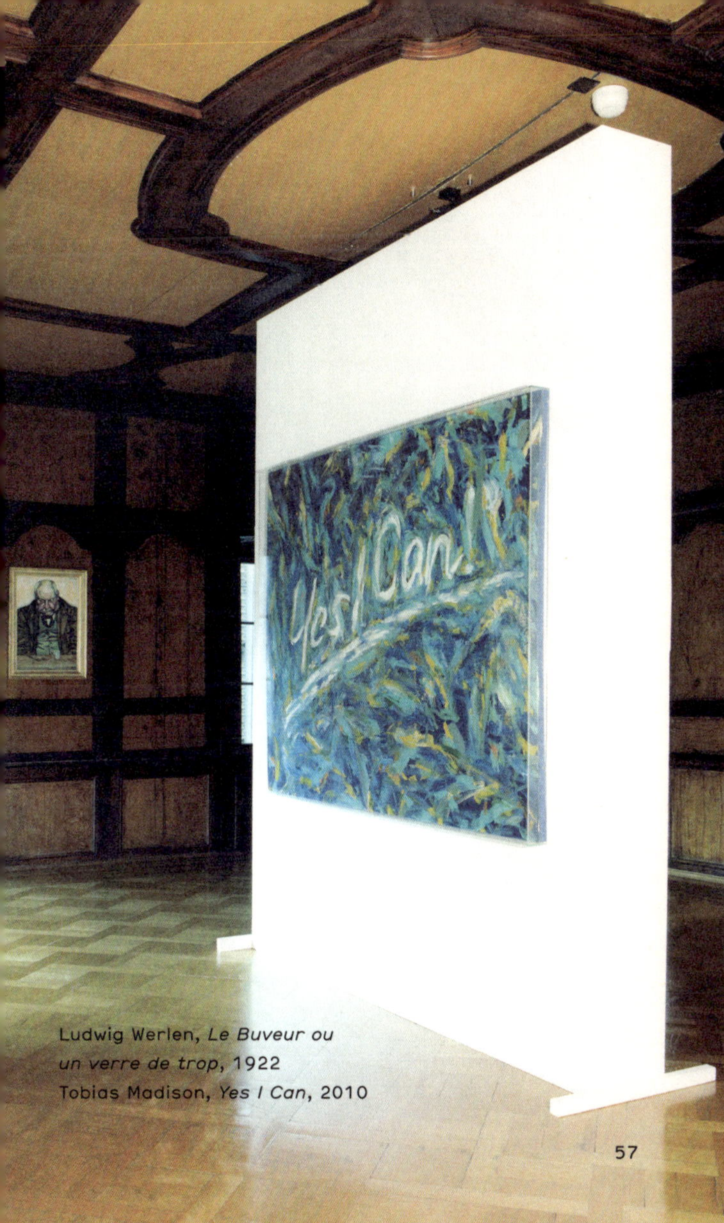

Ludwig Werlen, *Le Buveur ou
un verre de trop*, 1922
Tobias Madison, *Yes I Can*, 2010

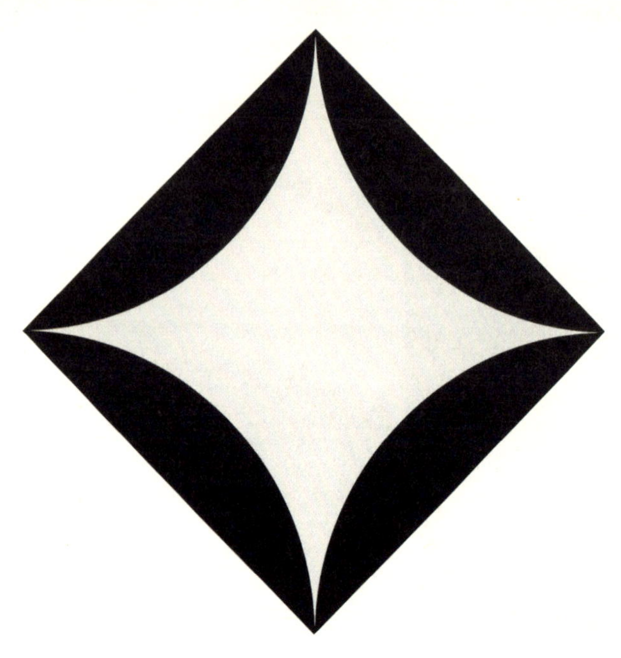

Stéphane Dafflon, *AST132*, 2009
Mirza Zwissig, *OCO*, 1973–1974 →

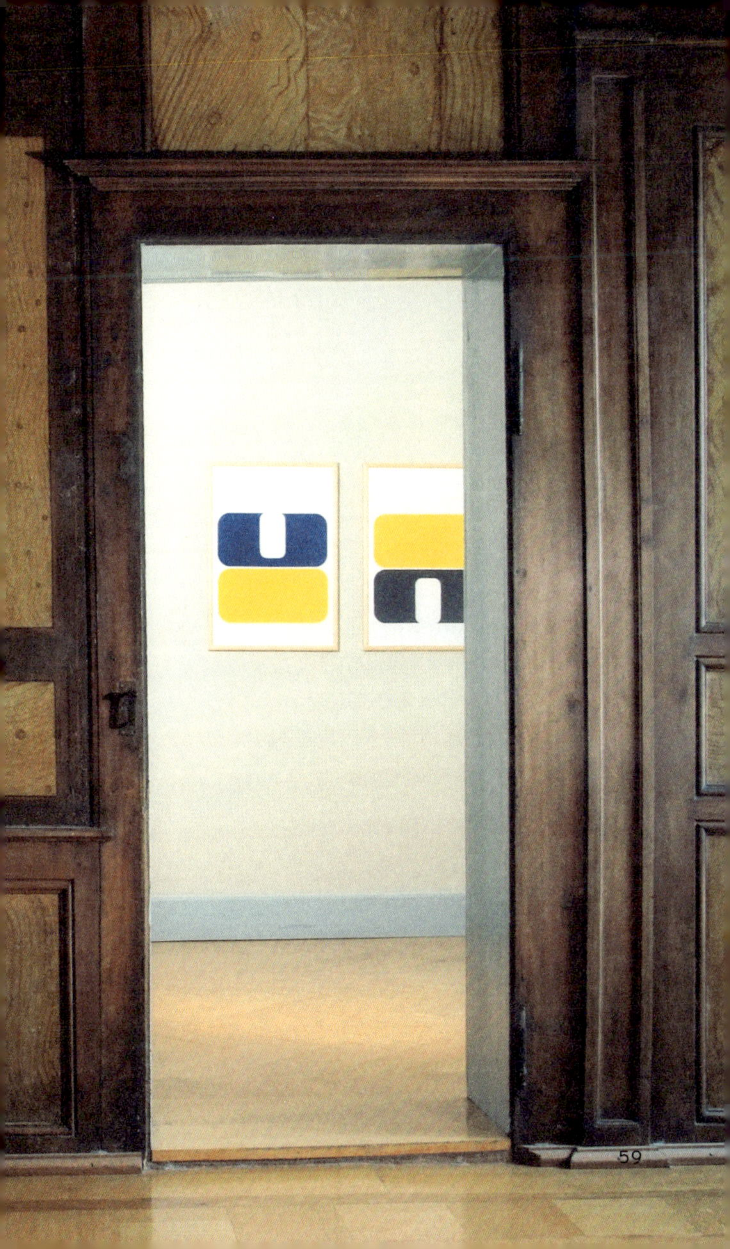

Exhibition view, "A Forest of Signs" section

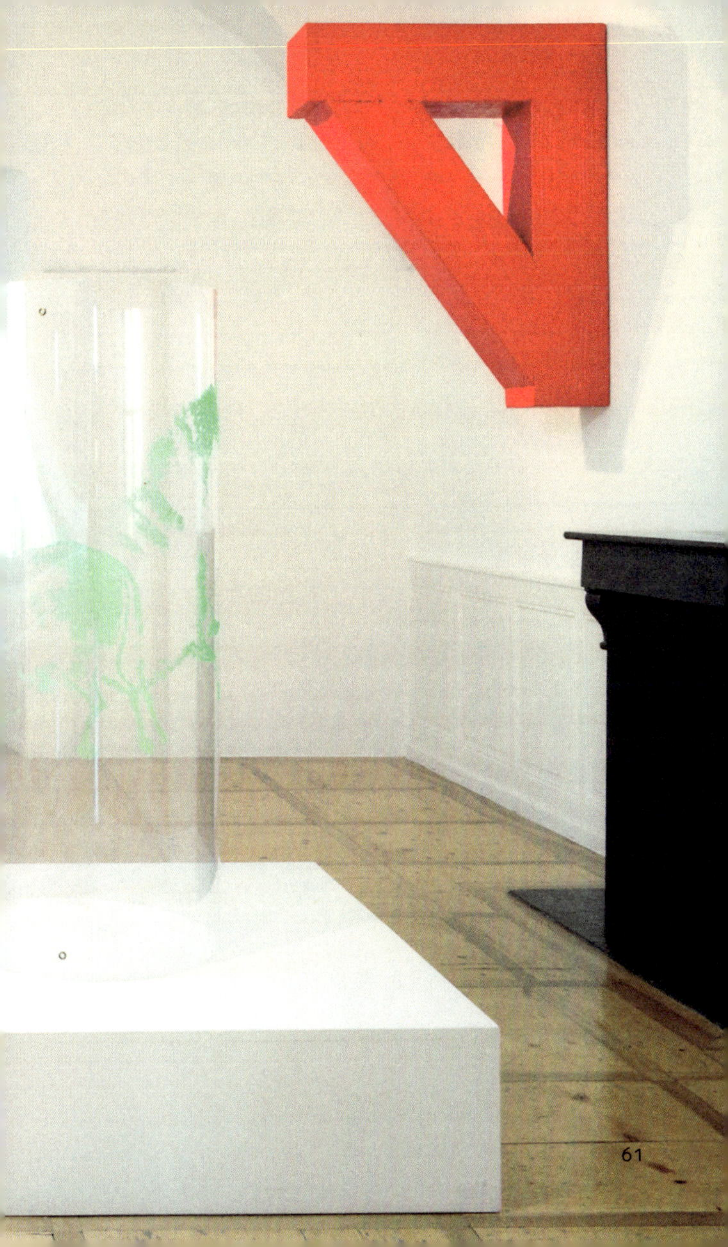

This book is published on the occasion of the exhibition *Aventures, reflets et embuscades – Adventures, Reflections, and Ambushes*, held at the Manoir de la Ville de Martigny, Switzerland, from September 4 through October 16, 2011.

Curator and Editor
BALTHAZAR LOVAY

Editorial Coordination
CLÉMENT DIRIÉ

Translation
SANDRA REID

Proofreading
CLARE MANCHESTER

Design
NICOLAS EIGENHEER, Zurich

Cover Image
AGNES RIEDER WILER,
Carnival mask from the Lötschental
Valley, circa 1980

Page 64
DAVID SHRIGLEY, *Untitled
(Relax In Peace)*, 2010

Photo Credits
JULIE LANGENEGGER

Color Separation and Print
MUSUMECI S.P.A., Quart (Aosta)

Typeface
HERMES-SANS (www.optimo.ch)

This book is published with the support of
LE MANOIR DE LA VILLE DE MARTIGNY
www.manoir-martigny.ch

It has received generous help from
BFAS, BLONDEAU FINE ART SERVICES,
Geneva
LA VILLE DE MARTIGNY
L'ETAT DU VALAIS

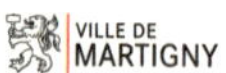

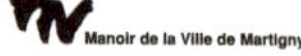

The editor would like to thank Daniel Baumann, Delphine Besse, Marc Blondeau, Valentin Carron, Claude Cortinovis, Philippe Davet, Véronique Gay, Samuel Gross, Mads Olesen, Mai-Thu Perret, Stéphane Ribordy, Marta Riniker-Radich, Céline Roduit, and Fabrice Stroun.

© 2012, the authors, the
photographer, and JRP|Ringier
Kunstverlag AG

Printed in Europe

Published by

JRP|Ringier
Letzigraben 134
CH-8047 Zurich
T +41 (0) 43 311 27 50
F +41 (0) 43 311 27 51
www.jrp-ringier.com
info@jrp-ringier.com

ISBN 978-3-03764-284-9

JRP|Ringier books are available
internationally at selected
bookstores and from the following
distribution partners:

SWITZERLAND
AVA Verlagsauslieferung AG
Centralweg 16
CH-8910 Affoltern A.A.
verlagsservice@ava.ch
www.ava.ch

FRANCE
Les presses du réel
35 rue Colson, F-21000 Dijon
info@lespressesdureel.com
www.lespressesdureel.com

GERMANY AND AUSTRIA
Vice Versa Vertrieb
Immanuelkirchstrasse 12
D-10405 Berlin
info@vice-versa-vertrieb.de
www.vice-versa-vertrieb.de

UK AND OTHER EUROPEAN COUNTRIES
Cornerhouse Publications
70 Oxford Street
UK-Manchester M1 5NH
publications@cornerhouse.org
www.cornerhouse.org/books

USA, CANADA, ASIA, AND AUSTRALIA
ARTBOOK|D.A.P.
155 Sixth Avenue, 2nd Floor
USA-New York, NY 10013
dap@dapinc.com, www.artbook.com

For a list of our partner bookshops
or for any general questions,
please contact JRP|Ringier directly
at info@jrp-ringier.com, or visit
our homepage www.jrp-ringier.com
for further information about
our program.

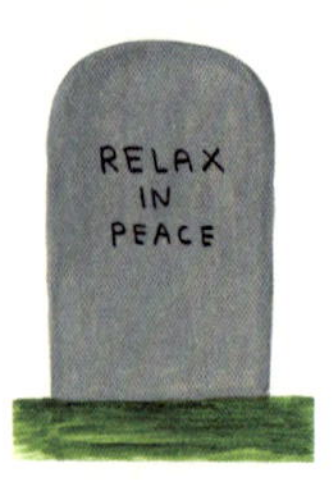

In the same series:

NICOLAS TREMBLEY (ED.)
Sgrafo vs Fat Lava (2012, English Edition)
ISBN 978-3-03764-277-1

WILLIAM POPE.L
Black People Are Cropped (2012)
ISBN 978-3-03764-269-6